WORKING FOR THE GREATER GOOD OF ALL ... REALLY

How my search for purpose in life
became my journey of faith

By Ken Lanci
with Manya Chylinski

A Smart Business Network Inc. imprint

Martin Luther King, Jr.'s *The Dimensions of a Complete Life* © The
Martin Luther King, Jr. Center for Nonviolent Social Change,
Atlanta, GA.

Bible quotations from New American Standard Bible

For information and inquiries, address:
Smart Business Network,
835 Sharon Drive,
Westlake, Ohio 44145
or call (800) 988-4726.

Cover design by Stacy Vickroy / Amanda Horvath
Layout and design by Kaelyn Hrabak
Edited by Randy Wood & Dustin S. Klein

ISBN: 978-0-9839983-5-8

Library of Congress Control Number: 2012952733

Contents

Preface

As you read this book, you will get a sense of me, my life and my goals. I am a believer in history and its lessons— lessons we should never forget nor the people who taught us those lessons.

When I began my political campaign, I went to see a friend, Carole Hoover, to seek her wisdom. She gave me a book written by Martin Luther King, Jr., *"The Measure of a Man."*

Carole could never have imagined what a profound impact she made on me with her gift.

Thank you, Carole!

I read the book that evening, and within its pages, I realized what Dr. King felt is what I was feeling. Then I knew that I must continue my journey *for the greater good of all.*

It is with this in mind that I reprint a few of the words uttered and written by the great man, himself, and the core of one of his messages for all of mankind. He states it so simply and elegantly, as only he could! I have included a few lines in the next pages, but have placed further reading in an appendix at the end of the book.

I hope you find his words as uplifting as I have.

KL

Excerpt from

"The Dimensions of a Complete Life"
by Martin Luther King, Jr.

"Many, many centuries ago, out on a lonely, obscure island called Patmos, a man by the name of John caught a vision of the new Jerusalem descending out of heaven from God. One of the greatest glories of this new city of God that John saw was its completeness. It was not partial and one-sided, but it was complete in all three of its dimensions. And so, in describing the city in the twenty-first chapter of the book of Revelation, John says this: 'The length and the breadth and the height of it are equal.' *In other words, this new city of God, this city of ideal humanity, is not an unbalanced entity but it is complete on all sides."*

King further explains: *"One day the psalmist looked up and noticed the vastness of the cosmic order. He noticed the infinite expanse of the solar system; he noticed the beautiful stars; he gazed at the moon with all its scintillating beauty, and he said in the midst of all of this,* "What is man?" *He comes forth with an answer:* "Thou hast made him a little lower than the angels, and crowned him with glory and honor."*

"[There] are the three dimensions of life, and without the three being correlated, working harmoniously together, life is incomplete. Life is something of a great triangle. At one angle stands the individual person, at the other angle stands other persons, and at the top stands the Supreme, Infinite Person, God. These three must meet in every individual life if that life is to be complete."

8

King goes on to write: *"The breadth of life is that dimension of life in which we are concerned about others. An individual has not started living until he can rise above the narrow confines of his individualistic concerns to the broader concerns of all humanity."*

So I say to you, seek God and discover him and make him a power in your life. Without him, all of our efforts turn to ashes and our sunrises into darkest nights. Without him, life is a meaningless drama with the decisive scenes missing. But with him, we are able to rise from the fatigue of despair to the buoyancy of hope. With him, we are able to rise from the midnight of desperation to the daybreak of joy. Saint Augustine was right—we were made for God and we will be restless until we find rest in him.

Love yourself, if that means rational, healthy, and moral self-interest. You are commanded to do that. That is the length of life. Love your neighbor as you love yourself. You are commanded to do that. That is the breadth of life. But never forget that there is a first and even greater commandment, "Love the Lord thy God with all thy heart and all thy soul and all thy mind." This is the height of life. And when you do this, you live the complete life.

What more needs to be said? As you continue to read my story, understand that my life up until dying, was the first two legs. And as King describes the third leg, he makes it clear to me how I have to complete my life.

Introduction

It feels strange to write a book about my life. I have always been a private guy—the kind of man who likes to keep things close to the vest. But now, I am involved in the community and have a public persona. I decided it is important to share my story so that people can understand who I am and why I do what I do. More important, I want people to understand why my mission in life is to achieve the greater good for all. Really.

Many years ago, in conversations with my good friend, Joe, we started the habit of qualifying each other's statements with the words, *"In my opinion."*

We realized and agreed that most coverstations were based on how someone percieved the information to be. Therefore the qulaifier was, *"Yes, that is in my opinion."*

From then on, unless I, he, or others, were making statements of fact, what we were saying was simply how we, in our opinion, were seeing the situation. That is the qualifier for this book as well.

This is a book about my life—from my perspective. When I talk about things and people and situations, what you are reading is my opinion of them. Some facts cannot be disputed, of course. But at times what I discuss here is my opinion—my view of the world around me. It bothers me that these days, too many things are written as fact—and people just accept that they are facts, even though they are really just someone's opinion. So I want it to be clear up front that what you will read in this book is a smattering of factual information and a collection of my opinions on how I see the world.

I will tell you what it was like to die and start life anew. It is important that you understand the impact that dying had on my life, as well as how it led to my current journey of faith.

I will discuss my 2010 run for Cuyahoga County executive in Ohio. I owed it to God and myself to do something different with the new life He gave me the day I died. Running for office was where the journey took me.

My life, the campaign, this book … they lay out how I've come to the conclusion that I can and want to make a difference in my community. They explain why I believe I am supposed to make a difference and should—for that is the reason I survived that day when I died. In these pages, I'll discuss how grateful I am for what I have had in my life and for the second chance I've been given.

Like any tough choice, deciding to run for political office was difficult. I wrestled with it for weeks. Up until then, I had lived my life in a way where I was taught that you didn't talk about who you were or what you had done. While growing up, it was never about me; it was always about others. But things are very different in politics. To help people understand what you stand for, you have to be able to tell people who you are and what you've done. You have to sell yourself—whether you like it or not. Politics have always been popularity contests. I'm still not comfortable with putting myself first, but now at least I understand that it is all part of the game.

This is a relatively short book—by intention. I've recognized that many books are "tell-all, be-all" pieces that go on for too long about parts of a person's life that few people care about. In my case, this book is not intended to be all-inclusive. Instead, I decided to put into words only what I thought was important enough to know about me in order to understand what my mission in life is really about. In this way, I hope you'll come to know me a little bit better. And now that I have been given that second chance, my personal mission is to remain steadfast to the path I'm meant to be on—working for the greater good of all.

So with that in mind, I am humbled to share this story about me with you. It's who I am, in my opinion, and what I believe in. I've bared my soul—good and bad—in order to be honest about my life. I owe you at least that much.

Through it all, I've come to learn one truism: What you are is God's gift to you; what you do with yourself is your gift to God.

Thank you for joining me on this journey.

Chapter 1

Working For the Greater Good of All

"Nonviolence means avoiding not only external physical violence but also internal violence of spirit. You not only refuse to shoot a man, but you refuse to hate him."
— Martin Luther King, Jr.

The last thing you want in life is to have an opportunity present itself and you don't know what to do with it. Running for county executive was the opportunity for me to do the best work to serve people in need. I didn't win.

The election results said to me that the political system remains broken. The way to get elections and politics back on track is to take the money away from them. The only way that will happen is if people start a movement to force Democrats and Republicans to work together to pass campaign finance reform that is fair and makes sense. If they don't, we vote them out and make office-holding a revolving door until we get people who will pass that reform.

People, we have to take a stand. Somebody, somehow, someday has to take the power back. The power is the vote. A vote should be a one-to-one thing. I have one vote. You have one vote. A billionaire has one vote. No one should get an advantage over anyone else for donating money.

We've got to stop the tons of money flowing into elections. Look at the 2012 presidential election The final price tag was more than $2 billion. Say that spending is capped at $250 million per candidate. That would save $1.5 billion. Spending money isn't the answer. It isn't working.

That's the big takeaway that I learned from my experience as a political candidate. And it's a pretty big lesson. It also served as a good time to re-evaluate my life.

If I look at a snapshot of who I am today and who I was at 18, would my life have been better if I'd gone to college? I like to think that had I gone to college it would have opened up different opportunities. But I am an individual who worked hard and didn't get to do a lot of things. My life surely would have been much different if I had attended college.

When I speak to students in schools, I tell them that they are learning 24 hours a day. Anytime you are awake, you are learning. You just have to look at it that way. Life is not about fun and games. Fun and games are things you do when you have the extra money and time to do them. But most of us have to work. This is what I learned by listening and paying attention to other people. That is one of the greatest lessons for any of us.

The most important way to be successful in life is to choose something you like to do, that you are good at, then immerse yourself in it. Work with someone in that field who is considered the best at it and learn from them. Or, if you have the ability, learn on your own. Today, with the Internet as a valuable resource, we have the opportunity to educate ourselves about so many different things. There is no limit on how to use your time if you have ambition and encouragement. What you choose to do with your life now, will determine your future.

To me, success is not about how much money you leave behind. It is about your ability to help others to do well, to help your children, to help your family, to provide more opportunities for the next generation. If you do that, you are very successful.

Who you are is the sum total of your life experiences. We all have our memories. We know how we evolved, even if we can't see the whole picture. For me, I treat people the way I expect to be treated. For those much less fortunate, I feel, *"There but for the grace of God go I."*

I've had ups and downs. I've lost a lot of money and had to start over. I don't take any of this for granted. None of us is ever very far away from where we started.

In some ways, I still have that weird feeling that I'm not actually capable of achieving what I have achieved. When I was a kid, maybe 8, 9 or 10 years old, I had insecurities like any kid. I walked alone sometimes and felt alone and wondered who my friends were. I never imagined I could have a life like this.

Part of what helped me become a success is that I had people who believed in me. Ralph Schlag, the banker who saw something in me and took a chance, giving me a loan to keep my business going when everyone else said no. When someone believes in me, I work to make sure I am worthy of their trust. I worked hard to earn Ralph's trust and to not let him down.

There were people I believed in, people I chose as role models. I didn't know the word mentor at the time, but I searched out people who I knew could give me guidance. Stanley and Art, my mentors, gave me the opportunity to see their lives, learn about them and what they were like, and to understand the way the business world operates. Together, these three men gave me an education I never could have received in college. They helped me become the man I am today.

Growing up, I had a lot of responsibility. Part of it was just who I was, who I still am, and part was the way my family was. I started working at age 8, and I've been working ever since. From that day on, I have been making money. I've been the responsible one in my family. People never really ask me to help them; they usually just seem to know I will. For most people, if I can, I will help. That has been true my whole life.

But that doesn't mean that those people, my family or anyone else, define who I am or what it means for me to be successful. One thing I believe is that you cannot let anyone else define your success or failure. You have to define that for yourself. Then put in the work to get to where you want to go. Success is not passed out like Halloween candy. No matter how hard you think you have to work to be a success, I am here to tell you that you that you have to work harder than that.

If you define success as making a living and having time for your family, then you can work 40 hours a week. If you define success as becoming financially independent, then you have to work much more than 40 hours a week. No matter what you think you see on TV or in magazines, you cannot make a lot of money without a lot of hard work.

Being financially successful also means getting inside the box. If you are outside the box and don't conform to some of what society requires and expects of you, you won't get anywhere. You won't be able to get in the box. That is just the way it is. Not my rule—it's the way it has always been. Success can be measured in many ways—being respected rather than feared is also success. A life devoted to others is success.

You take nothing with you when you die. That's one thing I know. There wasn't a U-Haul filled with money and useless things when I began my journey to feel all the love of God. And what a great feeling it is.

You don't have to conform, but then don't expect great success. When it comes to the box, there are acceptable and unacceptable ways to do things in business and in life. There isn't much you, or anyone, can do to change that. If you do things the acceptable way, you are in the box. If not, you're on the outside.

This is what I believe. It is my opinion about how to be successful. It doesn't matter where you started out life. If you started it without money or access or connections, it will be harder, but it is not impossible. Many hugely successful people in all walks of life have started from nothing. What matters is how hard you work and how much you want to be inside the box.

It is true that if you start out without connections and access, the way to get inside is to have someone give you a break. That isn't always easy, so you have to be on the lookout. Make your own connections. Emulate the behavior of people you want to be like. *"Fake it till you make it"* as some call it. Look for people who can be your mentors and ask them. Then, work hard to be worthy of their time and trust in you.

In my life, once I realized that there were opportunities not available to me because I was outside the box, I didn't throw my hands up and quit. I worked very hard to get inside. Now that I am here, I continue to work to make sure I stay inside. This is where the opportunities are. That is the choice that I have made—to work hard, to get inside the box, to provide for my family and others in need. I will continue to lift as many as I can and help them get into the box if they desire.

In general, life is all about choice, though not everyone gets a lot of say in the matter. Early on, I didn't necessarily have a lot of choices about what I did. I didn't go to college because I had to stay home to help out in the family business. I worked very hard and sacrificed time with my family to get in a position where I could provide what they needed. Later, after the hard work was put in, there were choices I could make about what to do, how hard to work, what kind of person to be. I am very happy with the choices I've made.

To me, the best choices I have made in my life were to marry Linda, have a family and to help others. That makes me feel good, and it helps improve the situation of people who may not have a lot of choices in their lives. Since my cardiac arrest, in most ways I don't feel I have a choice. I was brought back for a purpose, to help others. I was brought back to dedicate myself to serving the greater good of all. To the extent that I am here and can do something, I am going to do it.

After my cardiac arrest, I realized that we have very little control over what happens in our lives. Up until the day I died, I was never a risk taker. I was in the best physical shape of my life. I worked hard to provide for my family and many others. How could I die? It turns out that none of what you do really matters in the long run. When God wants you, He takes you. It really doesn't matter what you have done or what you plan to do.

Dying gave me the chance to decide what that moment meant and what I was going to do with it. I believe that to those whom much is given, much is expected. So every day, I am aware that I am here on earth, alive, to work for the greater good of all.

Getting involved with politics was not my choice. It was God's way of using the life I had been given back, for me to give back to the community.

Becoming a politician wasn't something I had any desire to do; it was never, never, ever my goal in life. I realized that running for county executive gave me the opportunity to have a voice. And to use that voice is the only way to make a difference.

As I've said, I think that politics and government in this country are screwed up. This is true on the national and local levels. We've become a nation of people with very low expectations of those who serve us. So, I am setting my expectations high. One person can make a difference. My message during the campaign was very simple: *"I am not a politician. I am the different choice you are looking for."*

I am who I am because of the sum of my life experiences. But, I am not that far from being the young boy I was when I lived in Morris Black Place, one of Cleveland's worst housing projects. There are things that bring back those memories sometimes. So, I don't take anything I have or anything I've earned, for granted. I could end up back there in a heartbeat. One of my greatest fears is that no one there now will have an opportunity to be successful.

When I was young, I don't know if I understood what success was or how to define it. I never imagined being successful, I just didn't think that way. Now that I am older, and I hope wiser, I define success as leaving the world a better place than when you found it. Whatever contribution you can make, do it. As MLK said, *"Do it as God almighty himself commanded it."*

And that is what it means to work for the greater good of all—really!

"But those who hope in the Lord will renew their strength.
They will soar on wings like eagles;
They will run and not grow weary,
They will walk and not be faint."

                                                — Isaiah 40:31

Chapter 2

Best Shape of My Life

"The stories of past courage can define that ingredient—they can teach, they can offer hope, they can provide inspiration. But they cannot supply courage itself. For this, each man must look into his own soul."

— John F. Kennedy

A tingling feeling crawled up my legs, moving slowly from my feet toward my groin. I looked at the doctor and said, *"I'm going out."* Then I died July 19, 2007. I was 57 years old.

For most people, death is the end. For me, however, dying was a turning point. My death was a gift. It was the birth of a new version of me, Ken Lanci 2.0. In a single moment, I was given the chance to learn again—about life, how to help others and how to develop a new me. My death reignited my passion for working toward fixing what needs to be fixed around me. Before my cardiac arrest, I was involved with many good causes. After, my eyes opened and I saw the bigger picture.

If I hadn't had a cardiac arrest and died, I would have continued to do what I'd always done. That's not a bad thing, but I would never have acquired the knowledge I have today. I would never have realized my mission in life. My journey of faith is to work for the greater good of all.

I would never have come to the conclusion that politics could be a path to help. Before the cardiac arrest, entering politics was something I absolutely would never, ever, ever do. But after my death, it changed things. I realized that maybe, just maybe, this was the path I was supposed to take.

Before I tell you about my experience in the world of politics, let me take a few steps back to where this all began. Let me explain what led to my death, even though at the time I was in the best shape of my life.

As an adult, I had the usual executive's life of no exercise —just a lot of work, work and more work. When I turned 44, I decided it was time to get in shape. I joined a gym, hired a personal trainer, Pat Ventre, and started power lifting weights. By the time I was 51 years old, I was competing competively and set a state of Ohio record for dead lift in my age group—465 pounds.

But that still didn't do it for me. Entrepreneurs are ultra-competitive, and I'm no exception. I turned my attention to bodybuilding, which requires a completely different workout and a diet focused on building muscle mass, and reducing body fat. After a few years, at the age of 54, I opted to compete and enter competitions.

Pat trained me for the previous 9 years. He led me through my power lifting and helped me revamp my workout and adjust to bodybuilding. My first workout with him, at age 44, was eye-opening —I benched 85 pounds.

It surprised me that the weight I could manage was so little, but I knew it was just a start. Under Pat's guidance, I began working out four days a week. We isolated my body parts, two each day, throughout the week and did repetitions to the point of fatigue.

My diet was comprised of protein and carbs—no fats. In time, my body fat was about 14 percent. For breakfast, I'd eat eight egg whites, a whole egg and a bowl of oatmeal. It was kind of bland, but I got into the zone and it was more than enough to satisfy my hunger. And I just felt good, real good.

If you've ever seen bodybuilders on television or in person, you've probably noticed their veins. Bodybuilders become very vascular—it's a sign of lean muscle mass. When you increase muscle mass, it puts more pressure on your body, and your veins stick out. This becomes a very visual result of the work. I could see that progress in me when I was working out, as well as after the workout was complete.

Yet, this was never quite enough for me.

Even as I progressed and saw my body change, I wasn't happy. Each week, I took a picture of myself to chart my progress and see which body parts needed improvement. Each time, I would think, *"I've got to do more; I've got to look better."*

About a month before that year's competition, I developed diverticulitis, a painful digestive disease. The diverticulitis was most likely a result of my new diet. It took awhile to get the diet right, but it also took me out of the competition.

I spent the next year working to get back in shape.

Six weeks before the competition I was in the best shape of my life. I had a 50-inch chest, a 33-inch waist, close to 9 percent body fat, and I could bench 375 pounds. I was ready to compete, and I was confident I was going to win. Hell, if I had to stand up in front of the crowd in a Speedo, I wasn't going to lose … or embarrass my family and myself.

One morning, I woke up not feeling well.

My arm hurt a bit. I had been working on the computer. Before I knew it, the pain increased. I put on my blood-pressure cuff to see if I could figure out what was happening.

My pressure was 270 over 135—double what it normally should have been.

I looked at my wife, Linda, and said, *"I think you need to call 911."*

A few minutes later, the emergency medical technicians arrived. They took an EKG and confirmed what I thought—I was having a heart attack.

The EMTs set me on a gurney, loaded me into the ambulance and drove me to Hillcrest Hospital with the sirens blaring. Luckily, it was less than a five-minute ride to the hospital from our house.

I was wheeled into the emergency room. Doctors and nurses were scrambling around me. Being the kind of person I am, the type who likes to be in control, I told them I'd get myself from the gurney to the bed.

After they got me settled into the bed, I looked into the doctor's eyes, had a cardiac arrest, and died.

The total time from calling 911 to being on the operating table and having a stent put into my heart was 67 minutes.

During surgery, the doctors discovered that my main artery, the LAD, or as it is commonly called, the *"widow maker,"* was 99 percent blocked. They found another artery with blockage. But I arrested again on the table, so they decided to leave that one alone.

Chuk-sssssssshhhhh.
Chuk-sssssssshhhhh.
Chuk-sssssssshhhhh.

Several hours after my death, I woke up in a fog.

The best way to describe it is that I was surprised and had some very alarming sensations. I knew that sound—the sound of a respirator—and then I thought, *"Someone's in big trouble."* I soon I realized it was me!

I couldn't swallow. I couldn't talk. It felt like I was suffocating.

My hands, legs and feet were tied down. I had a moment of panic and wondered, *"Do they even know I'm in here?"*

You hear stories about people who are on respirators, and the doctors that decide to pull the plug while they are still alive. I didn't want to become one of them.

I wondered again, *"Do they know I'm awake?"* And I tried to make letters in the air with my hand.

One of my daughters handed me a pad of paper. I scratched out, *"I'm OK."*

Everyone—the doctor, the nurses, Linda—was telling me I was OK. But what I meant was *"I'm OK. I'm in here."*

While all this was going on, Linda somehow kept her wits about her.

"I believe you are destined for a time," she says. *"God has it all marked out. Ken could have been at work when it happened, but on that day, we were going to golf with another couple. He could have been on a freeway, died, and stayed dead. But when he woke up and didn't feel well, things started to move fast, and you didn't have time to think."*

Being on a respirator, and being taken off of it, is not fun. I was never in control of anything going on around me. The respirator, for example, creates a feeling of suffocation. With a tube down my throat, my body regurgitated what was in my system—mucus and fluids came rushing out of my mouth and nose. It felt like it was oozing out of my eyes and ears as well.

That was a low point. Linda was there by my side.

"When they were rolling Ken through the hospital, he was awake," she says. *"So I got to kiss him before surgery. I didn't think anything until it was actually over. That's when you break down. You go in, you see him on the ventilator and think, 'I could have lost him.'"*

I am a type-A person, someone who is always in control; it was hard for me to let my body rest and heal. But, today's medicine is incredible. Even though putting in a stent is an invasive procedure, both the risk and recovery time are minimal. The next day, as I lay there in the hospital, it was hard to believe I'd gone through that experience. I mean, I was in great shape and felt pretty good. In fact, that morning, I felt the best I had in years. My heart was obviously getting more oxygen and getting more blood to my brain than it probably had been for a while. So it was a great feeling.

A few days later, they sent me home. I began my cardiac rehabilitation.

Think about that: I had a cardiac arrest and died, and I was only in the hospital for a few days! That is where modern medicine stands today. It's pretty incredible.

Before I resumed my regular workout, I asked the doctor about my long-term prognosis with weight lifting.

"Am I ever going to be able to lift heavy again?" I asked.

He looked at me and responded with a question of his own: *"Well, what's heavy?"*

"A couple of weeks before the cardiac arrest, I benched 375 pounds," I told him.

"Maybe you'll be able to do 370," he replied.

"Really?"

"Yeah, you're OK," he said. *"There was no heart damage."*

Despite this, that first month when I went back into the gym, I took it easy. I'd done cardiac exercises as cardiac rehabilitation, so I felt strong. I was good to go. I probably could have lifted heavier weights. But I decided to hold the party line and take things slowly. It's a good thing I did.

A few weeks later, after I had finished a workout at the gym—a light workout per doctor's orders—I was driving down the freeway on my way to meet a few friends for lunch. I started to get that feeling again: pain and tingling in my left arm and shoulder, as well as in my neck.

I was having another cardiac arrest. *"No way,"* I told myself. *"This is crazy. It can't be."*

I kept driving.

When I arrived at the restaurant, I was the first one there. I sat in the car waiting for my friends to arrive. Suddenly I thought, *"Why the hell am I sitting in the car? If I do have a cardiac arrest, nobody will know."*

It was a nice, sunny, Saturday in August, so I climbed out of my car and sat on a bench outside the restaurant. I decided to call my doctor.

He instructed me to take a nitroglycerin pill.

My doctor waited with me on the phone while the pill took effect. He asked how I felt.

"It feels a little better," I said.

"Take another."

The nitro caused blood to rush in my system and turned my face tomato red. While I sat there on the phone, my friend Andy arrived.

"What's the matter?" He asked.

"I'm fine," I said. *"I'm on the phone with my doctor."*

The second nitro pill made me feel even better, but my doctor was concerned.

"Get to the hospital," he told me. *"It might be another episode. The fact that the nitro took care of it is an indication it could be something. We need to get you checked out immediately."*

My doctor instructed me not to drive. He told me to have a friend take me to the hospital. Just as he was saying this, I heard sirens in the background, getting closer.

I turned to Andy, who shrugged. *"Your head looks like it is going to burst off your shoulders,"* he said. *"I wasn't going to wait."*

The ambulance arrived and whisked me off to the hospital.

My second cardiac arrest was caused by blockage in the diagonal artery—the one that they'd discovered in surgery and left alone. This time, I ended up at the Cleveland Clinic Main Campus.

There were a few more episodes over the months and weeks that followed.

First, I had pericarditis—swelling of the sac around the heart from being shocked. Then, a month later, I went back to the hospital because of chest pains. A month after that, it was more chest pains. It kept happening, over and over again. For the next seven months, I went to the hospital at least once a month.

I couldn't get rid of the pain. It would pop up out of nowhere. Sometimes, it would wake me up out of a sound sleep at 3 a.m. Each time, I would go to see the doctor. And each time, I was fine.

"I think I'm OK," I would say, *"But I'm getting tired of coming in."*

"No," they would tell me. *"You have to come in."*

"Well," I'd reply. *"I still feel stupid."*

"No," they'd say. *"The stupid ones are those who don't come in. And then for them, it's the end."*

I decided to stick with protocol.

The second cardiac arrest gave me pause. Even though they told me I was fine, it—combined with the pericarditis—made an imprint on my brain. The moment I would get a pain, any pain, I would react the same way: My brain took over and mimicked the pain of the first cardiac arrest.

Here I was, over and over, waking up at 2 a.m. and 3 a.m., with that same sinking feeling that I was having yet another cardiac arrest. But it was really just my brain repeating the symptom. What was happening was that I was unable to mentally process everything that had occurred.

After a year of this pain and of just not feeling right, I decided to go to a boot camp—30 days of working on the mind, body and soul. I met with a new doctor, who would be able to help me.

My brain was so imprinted that when I arrived I could not sleep alone in my condo for fear that I may need help and nobody was there. So, I hired a nurse to stay overnight. The first four days of the boot camp were hell. My body had a hard time adjusting, and I had a headache and was constantly sick to my stomach. After 10 days, I woke up. It was like flipping on a light switch. I was back to normal—and able to be alone.

Around the same time, I took a picture of myself. I wanted to see how my body compared to what it had looked like before the cardiac arrest.

It wasn't that bad at all. I kept my shape and didn't lose too much muscle or definition. I had gained four or five pounds. Then, before I knew it, I gained between 18 and 20 pounds. I would look at the pictures from my bodybuilding days, pictures that were never good enough for me at the time, and think, *"God, I'd give anything to look like that again."*

The first year after my cardiac arrest was extremely stressful. I needed to work hard to get my brain back in balance. I saw the doctor two to three times each week at the boot camp. After the third week, she said, *"I've got to give you credit. You have done really well. You've worked really hard in overcoming this."*

She worked to find a reason for my condition—something in my life, my family or business. But the only reason I was having trouble with my recovery was that my brain didn't understand that the episode was over and kept reliving the cardiac arrest. It needed a little jump-start to get past what had happened, it needed a push to get back to where it needed to be.

Two events during this time stand out for me. The first happened before the cardiac arrest; the other shortly after.

About three weeks before my first cardiac arrest, I was working out on my treadmill. It was morning, and I experienced a feeling I'd never had before on my left side. It scared the heck out of me.

I immediately made an appointment to see my doctor.

He conducted numerous tests and didn't see anything on the EKG. He referred me to a cardiologist, just to be sure.

I made the appointment to undergo a cardiac echo procedure.

"Your mother had a history of heart trouble," my doctor said. *"So let's do this."*

My medical insurance company, Medical Mutual, refused to approve the procedure the doctor prescribed. Despite the fact that it had been around for a while, Medical Mutual still considered it an experimental test.

My doctor resubmitted the request, explaining that the procedure was necessary. Medical Mutual refused it again.

Looking back, the strange part is that the insurance company didn't offer anything like, *"We don't cover that procedure, but we'll cover a cardiac catheterization instead."* If they had told me or my doctor that, I would have had it done, which would have been a very simple procedure. I would have been back to work in two days, and my life today would have been very different. I sued Medical Mutual—not for money—to change their decision on the cardiac echo procedure, so that in the future someone else who may not be as blessed as me can get the test when they need it.

In the long run, however, this wasn't meant to be.

It was divine intervention. I needed to have that cardiac arrest. This was something I had to go through in order to come out the other side with changed priorities.

At the time, business was going well. I had a great team on board, including my son, Wally, and two sons-in-law, Matt and Oliver. And my CFO, Terry Hartman, did what he always did —an outstanding job. There's a basic business tenet that says if you do a good job bringing talented people on board, you can make yourself obsolete. If you don't, then there will be plenty of turmoil and crisis and everything can go down the drain in your prolonged absence.

So on the day it turned out to be more than a fire drill, everyone who worked with me stepped up and did what they had to do. They didn't miss a beat, and I was very proud of them. The entire team performed extremely well during this difficult time.

A cardiac arrest is the kind of event that gives everyone pause. Everyone stops to think about the what-ifs, especially if you're the one who suffered the attack. But the truth is that I had no regrets. If that day had turned out differently—if I would have remained dead—I was good to go. I had no regrets about the things I'd done, about the life I'd led, the friendships I had, the family I raised, and the friends, family and community I had helped.

The reality is that I felt very blessed.

There's always more to do. You always want to do more. But given where I'd started from and where I ended up that day, I was good to go.

Yet here I was—given a second chance. After the cardiac arrest, I felt as if God was sending me a message. The message was this: I have always been extremely grateful for all that God has given me. I am a driven-committed person and God knows that. Not that I've been chosen for anything, but now that I have a second chance, this time around it isn't about me. Before the cardiac arrest, I focused on providing for my family, friends and the community. Now I understand it's about more than that. It's working for the great good of all—full time. So the journey began.

"What am I supposed to do?" I asked God.

I asked myself the same question over and over.

The answer I received was to focus on the greater good of all always. It's what I've been doing ever since.

Growing up, I was raised with the idea that when it's your time, it's your time. God makes the decision for you and nothing you do will change that. The irony is, however, that throughout my life I've made decisions that weren't necessarily in line with this belief.

When I was a 10 year old, I watched a watermelon fall off a table and burst. I realized that it didn't take much to bust open things that are soft, like a human head. So as a youth and young adult, I didn't take a lot of risks. I refused to ride a motorcycle, sky dive or use drugs and alcohol. I figured that if I avoided all those things, I would reduce my chances of dying. I foolishly believed that I could control when it would be my time.

Faith, I've learned, is a choice. I made my choice to have a relationship with God. When I was 19 years old, my best friend was a guy named Tommy. We planned to get married two weeks apart. I was going to be the best man at his wedding; he was going to be the best man at mine. And then Tommy died from a cerebral hemorrhage. Just like that, he was gone.

Before Tommy's death, dying really had little impact on me. He was the first person I was close with who died. It was a shock, and it caused me to question my faith. It made me ask *"Why?"*

In all the soul-searching that followed, I realized that everything happens for a reason. And it isn't our place to ask *"Why?"*

In my early twenties, I attended a gospel service for born-again Christians. Honestly, it just wasn't for me.

My feeling is that your faith is your faith. It's yours, alone. If someone asks you about it, you talk with them about why you made your decision and how you feel. You don't ridicule someone or try to get him or her to believe that he or she is doomed unless they make the same commitment as you—to be born again. That's just how I saw it.

In time, it made sense to me to make my own commitment to God—the type of commitment your godparents made for you as an infant.

When I was 23, our second daughter was born premature, at five and a half months. It had been a difficult pregnancy for Linda, and Theresa Rose was born weighing 1.5 pounds and was just 12 inches long.

Except for her lungs, she was fully developed—with fingers, toes and a little bit of hair. The doctors said she'd live for only eight hours. But Theresa Rose held on for longer. She was with us for 36 hours.

When Theresa Rose's body gave out and she died, I felt that she was in good hands. I felt that she was with my best friend, Tommy, and God would take care of her. I found comfort in that, in knowing that she was with God, and that ultimately, we will all be together again. My faith helped me get through this tough time.

I learned from Theresa Rose's death that God's message was simple and clear: When it's your time, it's your time. I will take you. You have no control.

So there I was, in the best shape of my life. I mean absolutely the best shape I'd ever been in, which I had controlled to get there. Then I had a cardiac arrest and died.

After I woke up, I realized that I had no control over any of the things in my life I thought I was managing. In the ambulance on the way to the hospital that morning, I never thought about it being the end. I remembered my religious training and made a confession, and said the Act of Contrition, so I would be ready if it was.

I didn't talk to God because I was in a crisis. Rather, I was doing the things I was taught growing up a Catholic. It's a little strange, given my doubts about organized religion, but at times like that, we all rationalize and want to cover the bases—just in case.

The prayers I said in the ambulance that day weren't three minutes too soon. In that moment, I saw the brightest light and felt the greatest feeling I'd ever felt. I had an absolute willingness and desire to just stay there. I desired to stay within the light and to experience the euphoric feeling I felt, a feeling I could not describe.

When I was campaigning, I told this story over and over. One evening, a gentleman approached me and said, *"I know that feeling. I was shot two times, saw the light and felt the same feeling."*

I told him it was difficult to explain.

He said, *"I know what it was."*
"Tell me?" I asked.

"It was the feeling of all the love of God," he explained.

"Amen," I said,

There is no other feeling I've ever had that was as good as the feeling I had that day—despite being dead. And I don't expect I'll feel it again until my time comes around for good. Phenomenal, fantastic, angelic, euphoric—none of these words completely describe the feeling I had. If you have faith, if you believe, the feeling is exactly what you expect it will be. Based on how I was taught and the things I'd heard, it actually beat the expectation of what I thought being in the presence of God and feeling all of His love would be like.

After my surgery, as I came out of the morphine-induced sleep, I had to cope with everything that was happening to me and my body. When I finally had time to think about it, the experience was very clear in my mind. I asked myself, *"What do I remember?"*

I remember being wheeled into the emergency room. I remember dying and seeing the brightest white light I had ever seen and a feeling beyond words. I had a flash of being wheeled down the hall. Everyone was running, including Linda, alongside the gurney. They hadn't let her into the room, but she saw me arrest and have a seizure.

Later, Linda told me that my face was so red I looked like a tomato. After she saw that, a nurse rushed her away, and no one told her a thing while they took care of me.

I remember telling Linda, *"I love you. I love you,"* when they wheeled me out of the emergency room. But, from what she told me about that moment, the words were just in my mind.

Being in the hospital, and then recovering at home, was a very different experience. I'm not the type of individual who gets sick. I'm never the one who needs others to do things for me. That's just not my style. Rather, I have been the person who is always there for everybody else. I'm the person who is in control. I'm the person who makes decisions and gets things done. Vulnerability wasn't a good feeling at all for me; flowers arranged around the house, get well cards, gifts from good friends. It all felt odd.

There was never any doubt in my mind about my family and how we all felt about each other. They were all there to see me. For that, I am truly blessed. And that's why I wasn't sad to think that I could have stayed dead. I didn't need a second chance to do things right, to tell people how I felt about them.

Am I grateful to be alive? Absolutely!

It's a bonus. I get to see my grandchildren grow up and share the love and blessings that God has given me.

If I had stayed dead that day, I was good to go. I had done everything I wanted to with my family, friends and business. Dying didn't really change the person I was inside. But, it did tell me in a very loud voice, I had to do something different. That's why I have dedicated my life to working toward the greater good of all and not just those around me.

"And without faith it is impossible to please God, for whoever would approach him must believe that he exists and that he rewards those who seek him."

— Hebrews 11:6

Chapter 3

Helping Others

"Children are the world's most valuable resource and its best hope for the future."

— John F. Kennedy

Some of my earliest childhood memories of are of my mother helping others—friends who came over for a meal, friends to whom she loaned clothes, even though she didn't have much to loan. I remember one girl, in particular, who was going to a dance. It might have been her prom. My mother had a party dress, and she let the young girl use it. No questions asked.

That moment was a very powerful one for me. It's burned in my memory. The girl was so grateful to my mom and my mom was so excited to let her use the dress that it became a special moment the two of them shared. It taught me that whatever you have, no matter how much or how little, you can make someone who is less fortunate than you happy.

From my mom's examples, I discovered our DNA was a match. I have dedicated myself to always helping others. It never occurred to me that there was an option. I didn't know you weren't supposed to. To me it was simple: If you can, you do.

A lot of people believe that if they don't have money, they can't help. That couldn't be further from the truth. Giving your time is actually the greatest gift. If we, as a society, understood how much giving time makes a difference, how good it makes you feel, more people would participate.

When I got to a point in my life where my time became more valuable than money, I made sure to provide my own labor to the causes I supported. After my cardiac arrest, I stepped up my efforts.

Philanthropy is a very personal decision. Don't misunderstand; we need people to give money. We are at a point in time in this country where needs are far greater than they've ever been. We need to focus our foundations and the people who have the financial resources toward helping people transition from this crisis so that they're able to make a soft landing.

Working with children in need is special because they are our future. No matter what you or I may do, if our schools can't prepare children for the next generation of the workforce, then we're all in trouble. This is happening in every community, not just the Cleveland area.

Rather than sit back and complain, Linda and I are trying to do something about it. I have gotten to the point in my life where I can. I believe that to those to whom much is given, much is expected.

The first time we gave money to an organization I was in my late 30s. Linda and I had been attending the same church since we were married. They organized a pledge drive to raise money to add a school. Our kids went to the local public school, but we value the importance of a good Catholic education.

Linda and I decided we would make a significant contribution to the pledge drive in memory of our daughter, Theresa Rose. They used the money for the kindergarten classes.

The pastor wanted to have a reception and a plaque dedicated to our daughter, but we never got around to it. We felt it was more significant for our family to know what we did rather than to advertise it for everyone else to see.

This is how we lived before I got involved with politics—things were contained and shared only among my family, God and me.

Things are different now. I have a much broader perspective.

One of the greatest satisfactions in my life is the ability to put a smile on someone else's face. It's instant gratification. Giving to organizations that have long-term benefits for others is a very good thing. For me, there is nothing quite like putting a pair of glasses on a child's eyes and watching them see clearly for the first time. When that happened, it grabbed my heart.

Until that moment, I never thought that the ability to see clearly was a problem for children. After all, this is 21st-century America. I was under the impression that if you were on public assistance and you needed glasses, you got them when you needed them.

That is not the case.

What I found is that there are only certain times when you are allowed to get glasses, and if you break them, you don't get another pair. Because of this, children can go two or three years without being able to see clearly. To me, this seemed criminal.

The Luxottica Corporation is one of my clients. Each year, they solicit vendors to raise money for its philanthropic foundation, OneSight, which provides free eye exams and glasses to children in need. In 2004, we contributed.

I had never heard of the program, but I liked their mission.

Linda and I made a gift to the foundation, and were invited to work at one of its clinics for a week, alongside its employees. It is an opportunity to see and experience the good works firsthand. Linda and I chose to work for a week in Chicago.

The process involves a nine-point eye exam, with eight of the stations staffed by volunteers. The employees taught us how to provide the exam—tasks they could teach the average person how to do—which included testing for color blindness and depth perception.

On our first day, we saw 500 children. More than 80 percent of them ended up needing eyeglasses.

The final station is where the kids see the eye doctor. He looks at the results of all the exams and decides if the child needs a full eye exam. Many of them end up needing glasses.

One of the great things about the program is that the children get to pick out their own frames—frames they like. Luxottica provides designer frames from among their brands because they know that kids won't wear glasses if they don't think they look good in them. So the children get to select from brands like Dolce & Gabbana, Oakley and Donna Karan.

When the kids find a pair of frames they like, their faces light up. The glasses are made that day and delivered the next. After our first day there, I said to Linda, *"I never realized there were kids that can't see. We have to get this in Cleveland."*

Today, we host the program. The first year, we provided eye exams for more than 700 kids. Since then, we've helped more than 12,000 children receive the gift of sight. My goal is to establish a permanent clinic in Cleveland.

"When Ken says something, he follows through," explains Linda. *"That's another one of Ken's great qualities. Some people say they'll do it, but Ken actually does."*

There is no substitute for having your wife support your endeavors, and Linda sees the importance of philanthropy the same way I do.

"Ken will sit down with anybody—even if they're having problems at home," Linda says. *"He'll sit down and give them a scenario to look at. I think it's a God-given talent."*

This has been my calling—helping others. When I was in a position to be able to help people, I began supporting an organization called Project Love. It is a character-building, education and training organization that works with teens and adults nationwide. Even though its focus is on more than just inner-city schools, working with Project Love helped me recognize how bad things are in the inner cities.

Project Love was founded by Susan and Stuart Muszynski, the daughter and son-in-law of my mentor, Stanley Yulish. Stuart started Project Love after a long illness where he learned about healing with love. His philosophy is that you can't always change your environment, but you can be your own rescuer. I've been involved since the early stages of Project Love.

The goal of Project Love is to help kids improve themselves and show them that they have control over how they respond to situations. It fits nicely with my life philosophy of helping others achieve the greater good. Over the years, I've been involved with Project Love in different ways—providing services, loaning money, donating money. In some cases, in lieu of taking fees from some clients, I ask them to write a check to Project Love.

"We both had a very passionate attitude about helping children" explains Stuart. *"Ken's attitude was that kids can be their own rescuer. That comes from his family circumstances. And he really identified with the messages that we were sending kids."*

Death taught me a lot about myself. Most important, it taught me that when I give to charities or do something for them, it should make a difference in someone else's life. Yet there are times when the problems are so big that it doesn't always seem that way. In 2008, Stuart and his wife, Susan, launched the Believe to Achieve program inside Project Love.

Their idea was pretty straightforward: There are a lot of inner-city high-school girls at risk. Their graduation rate is approximately 29 percent. In one Project Love school, they identified more than 70 at-risk ninth-grade girls and started this program to provide the girls with skills, faith, hope, love and the support needed to be successful.

Believe to Achieve's results are remarkable.

In June 2012, I attended the Collinwood High School graduation ceremony. The graduation rate for girls who went through the Believe to Achieve program was nearly 80 percent—that's compared to the average for all students at the school at 55 percent. Thirty-seven of our graduated enrolled in college. The next year, Project Love's graduation rate increased to 84 percent. These young women have transformed their lives. They believe in their own abilities and don't allow others to dictate their futures for them.

Project Love and Believe to Achieve—these are programs we know work. Now my goal is to get organizations and people in Cleveland to step up and fund this type of program so we can replicate it in all the schools in the Cleveland Metropolitan School District. This can serve as a model for the entire county.

"Relationships are always the driving force with Ken," Stuart says. *"They're very important to him. And what really drove Ken's passion about Project Love is that through it, he was going to help kids improve themselves, and it would help improve the schools as part of it. Ken would be able to help kids realize that there is a way of life where you can build others up, build relationships and promote kindness, love, understanding and collaboration."*

Not long ago, I read a statistic about people who experienced what I did. Less than 6 percent of people who have the kind of cardiac arrest I had survive it. There is a very short period of time when you can be saved. My doctor explained it is about 60 seconds without circulation to the brain and four minutes maximum before irreversible damage is done.

Given these odds, the question that lingered after I was brought back to life was *"Why me?"*

There had to be a reason. Not only did I survive a massive cardiac arrest, but I did so with no heart damage and with more energy that I had before.

God wouldn't have kicked me back to life in great shape without having a reason. And I've been asking myself ever since, what exactly am I supposed to do with this second chance?

"Ken's a faith-based person," Stuart says. "He believes that God gave him a mission in this world to do what he's doing and to help people. And if you believe God has given you a mission and that God is in charge, you follow. I think that is what has led him to the conclusion that he's put on this world to work for the greater good of all."

Despite my commitment to giving back and striving to achieve the greater good for all, I've made my share of mistakes in life. I'm no angel. But as a result of doing stupid things, all of us grow up and mature. We become adults, and our existence becomes the sum total of our life experiences. It is what defines us. When I look at what I've accomplished and the blessings I have—family, friends, grandchildren—it's far more than I ever expected.

"Ken has taken the concept of love and put it in some real pragmatic terms," Stuart says. "It's a process ... and it's wonderful."

I've been able to love. I've been loved. I've been able to help people. I've been helped. If it had been the end, I was good to go. I didn't have things I needed to take care of. So why am I still here? What am I supposed to do? People told me that I would know what I was supposed to do when it presented itself to me.

It was the passage of Issue 6 in 2009, when the voters of Cuyahoga County in Ohio approved a new charter to change the head of the county government from three commissioners to a single executive.

When I saw the qualifications for the county executive, they were everything I had done for the past 30 years: merging offices, turning around a culture, starting up out of the ashes of failed organizations. It was too much of a coincidence that things were happening this way. Do I believe or not? I flat out said, *"No."*

Several people told me this is what I should do.

"No!" "No!" "No!" I replied each time.

Then one morning, I woke up and thought, *"Oh boy. Maybe this is what I'm supposed to do—something I would never, never, never do."*

I got it!

That is when the whole idea of working for the greater good of all became my true focus.

My life wasn't going to be about me anymore. It was about what I could and would do with the gifts I had been blessed with, the resources at my disposal and the skills I could bring to bear. It was about the fact that I had an obligation to put in the time and effort to create change. And it was about the fact that I was able to utilize skills that other people didn't have, and use them for the benefit of all.

When I finally decided to run for office, I wrestled with having to talk about what I had done in my life and my business. My political advisers said that if I entered politics I would have to tell people who I am and what I've done.

In politics, you have to build credibility. It's truly a popularity contest. People want to know who you are, what you stand for and what you are doing. That's the game. And you have to be willing to sell yourself—whether you like it or not. And more often than not, the best candidate does not always win.

Playing the political game is a double-edged sword. I am not comfortable talking about myself, but I understand that it is part of the rules. So, I decided to put myself out there. It was the way God chose for me to be able to work for the greater good of all.

"What good is it, my brothers, if a man claims to have faith but has no deeds? Can such faith save him? Suppose a brother or sister is without clothes or daily food. If one of you says to him, 'Go, I wish you well; keep warm and well fed,' but does nothing about his physical needs, what good is it? In the same way, faith by itself, if it is not accomplished by action, is dead."

— James 2:14-17

Chapter 4

If You Always Do What You've Always Done, You'll Always Get the Same Results

"Take the first step in faith. You don't have to see the whole staircase, just take the first step."
— Martin Luther King, Jr.

OK, God. I understand. When you want me, you'll take me. But it wasn't my time yet.

Before my cardiac arrest, I believed that you had some level of control over your own life. Some of it was in your hands. Then, all of I sudden, I was dead. And, after I recovered. I realized I was wrong.

"How could this happen to me?" I asked myself. I was in the best shape of my life, not taking risks, not doing things that could jeopardize my health. I had done a lot of things right, a lot of things that should, in my opinion, qualify me for a longer period of time on this earth.

But doing things right doesn't entitle you to any extra time. When He wants you, He will take you. And it's not for us to question why. That, in a nutshell, is my opinion about life and death, and everyone is entitled to their own opinion. For me, the proof is in the process. The process was that I did as much as I could to take control of my life, to increase my changes of living a long life, and at that one moment, it didn't matter.

If I could talk to my 20 year old self to suggest making any changes, I don't think I would change much. Perhaps the one thing I would have changed would have been to smoke less. I'm not sure I smoked more cigarettes per hour than was normal, but given the amount of hours I was awake, I smoked a lot.

I started smoking early, at age 7. My father smoked, so I had access to his cigarette butts. He smoked filtered cigarettes, and every now and then, there was one that was a little longer than the others. Eventually, my curiosity got the best of me. And there were also a couple of neighborhood girls I was trying to impress.

By the time I was 11 years old, I was a regular smoker. When I graduated high school, I smoked three packs a day. I was up to four packs a day when I got married. Eight years later, when Linda's father was diagnosed with cancer, I took him to Mexico for treatment. If I was going to this God-forsaken place in the mountains of Mexico to help him get better, I sure wasn't going to come back for myself later. That's when I quit smoking.

Timing was everything.

When I quit smoking, I had reached a point where I could barely breathe normally at night. Taking my father-in-law to the clinic in Mexico and seeing all the other sick people waiting in line was a real eye-opener. That reality, plus my physical condition, made it the perfect time to quit smoking after 21 years. I was 28 years old.

I had another aha moment after my cardiac arrest. I realized that I was no longer here for me. My family and I share a common gratitude and appreciation that I am still alive.

Until my kids became adults, they didn't have a clue about what it takes to balance parenthood and financial survival. Wally gets it now. My daughters? Maybe not as much. But my relationships with them didn't really change after the cardiac arrest. Our feelings and raw emotions were tested; our love for each other was never questioned. From my perspective, I am the one who really understands what a difference that day made. I felt all the love of God.

When most people go on vacation, they call in for the first three days, but after that, no one worries about it. It seems to me that three days is really all the impact we have in life. The first day, someone is not there, everything he or she was doing or was expected to do doesn't get done and people have to scramble.

The second day, the person calls in because there are still a few things to take care of. By the third day, most of what he or she was doing is reassigned to others. It's been my experience that when someone dies, the family goes to the funeral, does their grieving and after several days, life goes on as usual. People go back to work and get back to living.

That is the way it should be. Life is for the living.

In His infinite wisdom, God gave us the ability to grieve and to heal. That is normal. Thinking of myself as having died is a memory. It's not a whole lot different than remembering last Christmas. Last Christmas was happy, but it was sad when dad died. That's it. No dwelling. Keep the wonderful memories and don't let them go.

People don't dwell on other people's issues. We dwell on our own based on how it affected our life—good, bad or indifferent. When we have that aha moment—like the cardiac arrest—it's only really important to us because we have to decide what to do with it. What to do with the moment and the change it means? Do we respond to it? Do we embrace it? Do we stay true to it? Or do we do stay true to it for a short while, through convenience?

Living your life based on something that has happened to you in the past takes a conscious effort every day. Once you forget about what happened, as the memory of the experience softens, you tend to drift back to being the person you were before, back to the same habits, same routines.

That is why it is my vow and my mission not to forget what happened to me. Not to forget that I am living a second chance to do better and not to forget what I can do about it every day.

I've had this conversation with my close friends and family; they understand what I've come to believe and embraced it with me.

"Part of life's process is coming to understand the 'why,'" says Stuart Muszynski. *"That first summer and fall following Ken's cardiac arrest, he was struggling with the 'why.' He had to be reassured that he was brought back for a reason, that it was not random coincidence, and initially, he was even struggling with that."*

Every day, I do something to further the gift of being here—whether it is helping somebody or something or working toward the greater good. I am conscious of this effort every single day.

"When you approach life with a conviction of 'I know that this is right, and I know that this is what I'm supposed to be doing,' then you allow the little blips along the way to roll off your back because you know there's a bigger picture of what's guiding you," says Stuart. *"And I think that's the realization Ken has today."*

Stuart knows me well, but few people know me better than my executive assistant, Vickie Zak. Although she didn't know the full extent of my involvement in philanthropy, she has definitely noticed the difference in me from before the cardiac arrest to now.

"He was more 'all business' with appointments and people before the cardiac arrest," Vickie says. *"It was fine; that's what I was used to. But after the cardiac arrest, he's been trying to help everybody. He always cared about people. But he probably never had the opportunity to help so many others. So the more he did, the better it made him feel. The cardiac arrest really changed his perspective—he started caring about things even more."*

After the cardiac arrest, my aha moment was the decision to get involved in the bigger picture, to get involved in politics.

By then, I had been involved in the community for a very long time, giving my time and my treasure. But in terms of making an impact, at times I felt I was just peeing in the ocean. Was it really making a difference?

Politics is different. It provides an immediate voice. And you acquire that voice the moment you announce you are running for office. Suddenly, people want to hear what you have to say.

More important, I care about what others have to say. It's just who I am. I try to help whenever I can. My opportunity to do so is greater now than in the past because people will approach me. They feel that they kind of know me. So I try to help anyone who approaches. There will never be enough money to solve everything, but providing solutions and guiding someone is at times more valuable.

In my opinion, there are always solutions to whatever problems stand in the way of success. Over the years, I've hired people with troubled pasts and given them a second chance. People deserve that.

Looking back at everything that's happened to me—not just since my cardiac arrest but all the way back to my childhood—it is mind-boggling. It is beyond any expectation I could have ever imagined. I could not imagine even remotely accomplishing what I have accomplished. It was never my goal. My goal was just to work harder and do better and to take care of my family's needs.

As I mentioned before, my mother believed that charity began at home. If you were going to spend time and do something, make sure things are OK with your family before helping others. But mom did not always live that. She took care of things at home, but if someone else needed something, she would drop whatever she was doing and be right there.

I was 19 years old when I asked for Linda's hand in marriage. Her father said yes right away. Her mother? Not so fast! She asked me how I would provide. I told her I would provide Linda with all the necessities in life and as many of the luxuries as I could afford. There was no promise of luxuries. But all of her needs would be met. She would never have to worry. And she never did.

In terms of working for the greater good, not everyone is in a position to do so. I think that 99 percent of people in the world are busy doing things for their families. Those who can, do when called upon. I get involved, sometimes to a fault. That's my nature; it is who I am.

One of the great things about America, and it has been proven over and over, is that in a crisis Americans bond together for the cause of the greater good. It's just the unfortunate part of life that after we attack a problem and solve it, we get back to our lives and forget about it.

I have been blessed with a keen sense of diversity in my life in terms of people, business and lifestyle. I've been around. Embracing my gift gives me a unique perspective at solving problems and helping people through their issues. And if I don't know the answer, I send them to somebody who will help them get there. To me, that is what it means to work for the greater good of all.

And it's meant even more since I died … and came back to life.

"I was hungry and you gave me food, I was thirsty and you gave me drink, I was a stranger and you welcomed me, I was naked and you gave me clothing, I was sick and you took care of me, I was in prison and you visited me. Then the righteous will answer him, 'Lord, when was it that we saw you hungry and gave you food, or thirsty and gave you something to drink? And when was it that we saw you a stranger and welcomed you, or naked and gave you clothing? And when was it that we saw you sick or in prison and visited you?' And the king will answer them, 'Truly I tell you, just as you did it to one of the least of these who are members of my family, you did it to me.'"

— Matthew 25:35-40

Chapter 5

Family Matters

*"Love is patient; love is kind; love is not boastful or arrogant
or rude. It does not insist on its own way; it is not irritable or
resentful; it does not rejoice in wrongdoing, but rejoices in the
truth. It bears all things, believes all things, hopes all things,
endures all things."*

— I Corinthians 13:4-7

For the first four years of my life, I lived in a unit at Morris Black Place at 110th and Woodland. It was a two-story brick building in the projects on the east side of Cleveland. And it was our home.

Then we upgraded and moved into the lower level of a two-family home in Cleveland. The neighborhood was still pretty rough.

As a kid, I was inquisitive and kind of mischievous. One day when I was 7, I had some idle time and started a fire. I was a little infatuated with fire then and was alone in the bedroom with matches and some pretty white curtains. They were chiffon, if

I remember correctly. I struck a match and set the bottom of them on fire. They went up like flash paper.

Suddenly, I had to think: Do I just let them burn or do I tell someone?

Fortunately, my aunt was there. She threw water on them to put out the fire, which by then had reached the ceiling.

After the fire was out, my mother wanted to kill me. I had to think quickly. Telling her that I had intentionally lit the fire didn't seem to be a good idea. Instead, I told her that when I went to strike the match it burned my finger, so I threw it and it hit the curtain. I stuck with that story for a very long time.

That same year, there was an incident at my school with one of the nuns. She told me to clean the chalkboard and the erasers. They were those large, 18- to 24-inch rubber erasers, the finishing touch to get all the last dust off the board.

I went outside and tapped them on the side of the school building to clean them. Obviously, this put chalk dust all over the side of the building, but the erasers were clean.

Another nun came out, saw what I was doing, picked up the big eraser and starting hitting me with it. She wailed on me with the eraser. I didn't know what the hell I'd done wrong. Clearly, though, she didn't like the mess I had made on the bricks.

I had chalk dust all over my back, on the cute little navy blue jacket that I was wearing and on my white button-down shirt.

When she stopped hitting me, she said, *"Don't say anything to your mother."*

I was ready to go with that plan.

When I walked into the house covered in chalk, my mother asked me what was wrong. It probably looked like I had rolled in flour.

"Nothing happened," I said.

"What do you mean, 'nothing'?" she yelled.

So, before I got another beating, I gave up the nun.

Usually, I didn't get an ounce of sympathy about things like this. This was probably the only time in my life that my mother ever went to school and voiced displeasure.

When my mother was two years old, her mom passed away. The love of a mother was something she never had. It was something she only could imagine. She imagined it as all good, that there was never anything bad.

The pain of growing up without a mother drove my mother, and I think she overcompensated. She was extremely affectionate toward anybody and everybody, especially her kids.

My father was the exact opposite. He was not affectionate. My dad was happy to sit on the side and be the person you had to go to and show respect. He was an ex-Marine. He had a temper, but he also had a long fuse. So when he got angry, he really got angry.

At some point in my youth, I decided I was going to be different. I decided that when I had children, I would be affectionate. I would tell them that I loved them. I would not be detached.

I never liked getting smacked. I'd say, *"What's that for?"* And I'd never get an answer. I decided that when it came to disciplining my kids, I would do it so they would understand; I'd explain what they did wrong.

When I was 8 years old, we moved to a house in Maple Heights, a quiet suburb south of Cleveland. The last night we were in the two-family house in Cleveland, we slept on the floor because the beds were packed up and ready to move the next morning.

My last memory of living in that house was waking up to the sound of somebody screaming. It was my sister. There was a rat running by her. When you're in a bed, a rat scurrying by isn't a big deal. But my sister was on the floor and it freaked her out. Her screams woke us all up and made my mother crazy.

After we moved, my father got me a dog, a boxer named Queenie. She was a great dog. I love boxers. I was responsible for picking up the dog crap, which I was happy to do. From that point forward, from the time I was 8 until now, one or two boxers have always been in my life.

My dad was an artist; he had a gift. But he wasn't a worker. He was the proverbial starving artist and kind of lazy. Dad had a 10th grade education. That's the way things were. Before we moved to Maple Heights, we were living hand-to-mouth. When we moved, my grandmother gave my father and his brother some money for a down payment on a house. Her second husband, Dominic Nolasco, the grandfather I knew, died of a cardiac arrest and she had moved in with us.

Grandma lived on the second floor of our Maple Heights house. She had her own living room, bathroom and bedroom. It was a blessing to have her there.

Since she was his mother, my grandmother was able to manage my dad. While my grandmother was living with us, my father began to grow up—fast. He was 35 years old. Prior to that, my dad hadn't held a steady job. But when my grandmother was there every day, dad couldn't do what he wanted to do anymore. She sold her house and gave each of her sons some money for down payments on houses of their own. She put some money away for herself, too.

But even with the down payment, my dad had to start working full time. The funny part is that I think I understood all of this at the time—understood that my dad didn't have a steady job and what it did to the family.

My dad's effect on the family impacted my brother, Tom, in a much different way than it did me. Tom is eight years my senior. He was 16 years old when we moved to Maple Heights. In a normal household, one would expect the 16 year old to cut the grass and do the chores, but he never did. Instead, my father showed me how to do it, and it became my responsibility. I took out the garbage as well.

To make money, I was ready to do anything I could because I couldn't get anything from my parents. They didn't have any extra money.

When my brother's friends came over to the house, I would shine their shoes for money. I remember that on one Thanksgiving I actually washed their cars for money, even though it was cold outside. I washed them with a bucket full of water and towel-dried them. It was good to learn at a young age that if you work, you get paid, and if you want to get paid, you have to work.

It just started early for me; the responsibilities always fell to me. My brother didn't do chores and my sister was not very motivated either. My grandmother was a disciplinarian. She would tell my sister to wash the floor. After she finished the job, she would show her some dirt and tell her it wasn't clean enough. Then my sister would cry and I would feel bad. I'd end up washing the floor. I guess I was always the responsible one, the one then who ended up having to do whatever was required.

Maybe it was because I was the youngest. I'll never truly know for sure. We all have our DNA, and our environment does shape who we are. But it is also our own thoughts about what is happening around us. And I didn't like the consequence of not having money.

There were bill collectors who would come to the house and knock on the door. Mom wouldn't answer the door. My mom would make us get on the floor and lay down so the bill collectors wouldn't see we were home.

In 1963, when I was 13, my dad bought a printing business for $1. I remember this vividly. He was so excited and caught up in the idea that he could buy a business for a buck. My parents thought it was a gift from God.

I said to myself at the time, *"What is wrong with the business that he got it for a buck?"*

It just didn't make any sense to me. And I was right. My father bought a business that owed the IRS $25,000. He signed an agreement and didn't have any clue what it said. It took about 18 months for the problem to manifest itself, and he ended up bankrupt.

With the help of my father's lawyer, Stanley Yulish, he bought the company's assets back at auction. Stanley became a partner. The business was reorganized and started over. But it always operated on the brink of going broke.

Because of my circumstances, I became pretty mature for my age. Other third and fourth graders would go bowling on Saturdays. They would talk about it at school. I wished I could go, too, but I didn't have any money to go bowling. So when I was 8, I started shoveling snow for money. I charged 25 cents per driveway. It was easy money with no overhead expenses.

My first experience with negotiation was with a neighborhood grandmother. It was snowing and she had a very large driveway. I told her I wanted 75 cents to shovel her driveway. She said, *"No."*

"I'll do it for 50 cents," I said.

"Thirty-five," she offered.

"OK." I agreed.

It was still snowing when I finished, so I had to keep shoveling in order to keep her driveway clear. A normal driveway took about 30 minutes to shovel. Her driveway took me 1 ½ hours.

This was a valuable life lesson

When I was about 12 years old, I did odd jobs like cleaning attics and barns for people, wherever I could find some work. My first job working for a boss was working on an ice cream truck. And then, when I was 14, my cousin, Bob, gave me a job in a Thom McAn shoe store where he was the manager.

Those were the good old days when you could lie about your age. I made about 85 cents an hour, working a couple of nights a week and on Saturdays.

I got a job at Sears when I was 16. With that, plus my job at the shoe store, I was working every single night and on weekends. Later, I picked up another job working as a porter at Federal Department Stores in Cleveland. I worked there as a janitor, taking out the garbage, cleaning toilets and burning mountains of trash.

I met Linda at Federal. She worked there as a sales clerk. We went to the same high school but didn't have any classes together.

During my senior year of high school, I went to school plus worked a full day. I started the day at a doughnut shop from 5 a.m. to 8 a.m. It was right down the street from school, so afterward, I ran to school. My classes were from 8:10 a.m. to 11:00 a.m. Then I left school to go to my cooperative-education program, which was an unpaid position working in my dad's print shop. It was how I helped my family.

By noon each day, I'd be working. Then I would leave the shop at 5 p.m. to work at Federal's by 6 p.m. I was eventually promoted from porter to the housewares department.

After graduating from high school, I had hoped to go to college to become a doctor. But when I spoke with my brother, he told me, *"You can't leave."*

We came to the conclusion that my father would lose his business again if I left for college. I had been able to make a positive impact on my father's ability to keep a paycheck. Without me there to help keep the printing business going, my brother said, it would fall apart. So I dropped my plans to go to college to keep working with our dad.

"They always relied on Ken," explains Linda. *"It takes drive. You either have it in you to do this or you don't. If you have it in you, you will push no matter what. Ken just took charge. He's gifted that way."*

The end of the summer after graduation, I got into a car accident and was in the hospital for a week. The following spring I needed surgery because the abdominal injury I suffered was not healing. I couldn't work on the print shop floor anymore, so I moved into the office. That's when I realized that the business was a mess. We were virtually bankrupt again. Chalk one up for Tom's intuition.

Staying with my father to ensure his business remained viable was just one example of how the importance of family impacted my formative years. Spending time with my grandmother was another.

My grandmother bought a 1964 four-door Chevrolet Bel Air when I was a teenager. It was silver. It was cool. She didn't have a driver's license, but my father went with her to pick out the car.

It fell to me to teach my grandmother how to drive. She was 64 years old. I was 14.

As crazy as it sounds, I had been driving since I was 12 years old. I learned sitting in the backseat when my dad taught my mom to drive. I was paying attention. After that, I would take my grandmother and two of my buddies out and teach her how to drive. She was a hoot.

When I was 18 years old, my grandmother remarried for the third time and moved out of the house. Not long after, her husband died. She was a great lady. She never complained about anything. My routine was to see her on Saturdays. We'd have a bite to eat, spend some time together, and we'd talk. When I was ready to go, I'd walk down the hall and turn around and she would wave goodbye. She always stayed there until I turned the corner.

My grandmother died when she was 88 years old. She had gotten kidney cancer and moved in with my parents for the last two months of her life. I was with her when she died. It was remarkable. She had a second wind a few days before, as if she'd been healed. And within two days, she went downhill fast. I spent the last days with her.

On that last day, she mouthed, *"I love you."* I went into the kitchen to get something to drink. When I came back, she was gone.

My brother was close to my father. He was named after my grandfather, which was a tradition in our family. My grandfather, Tom Lanci, was a philanderer and a landscaper. I never knew him. He died of a number of things. Growing up, I never knew that my grandmother openly hated him.

His namesake, my brother, was first-born and received all the attention. When I was growing up, there wasn't one thing I liked about him. My relationship with my brother could be described one way—nonexistent. I was a gnat on an elephant's ass as far as Tom was concerned. He was always more interested in his friends and aloof with me.

Tom never had to do chores around the house. The only work he did as a kid was to get up early each day and drive my grandmother to the bus station so she could take the 5:30 a.m. bus downtown to go to work at Hough's Bakery.

Tom is a lot like my dad. But Tom's fuse was much shorter. If he got angry, he was really angry. Tom was spontaneous, though it seems he was always looking for a fight. He was that kind of guy. That didn't make any sense to me, even as a kid.

When we lived in Maple Heights, between the time I was 8 and 12, Tom and I shared a double bed. He would come home, punch me in the leg, and tell me to get on my own side. Consequently, I learned to stay on my side of the bed, but he would still punch me in the leg. He moved out when he was 20, when I was 12. Then I had the bedroom to myself, which was great.

My sister married when I was 19 years old. And I married Linda when we were 20. My sister divorced a few years later. She had three children. After the divorce, they moved in with my parents. It fell back on me to take care of my sister and her three kids.

Then, my brother Tom was indicted for aggravated murder. At that time, his wife was pregnant and needed help, too. I was always happy to do my best. God only gives you what you can handle. But, by now, I asked God to take a hard look at my pile.

My niece, Marie, my sister's oldest daughter, died from lupus at age 16. She developed a blood clot in her lung around Thanksgiving and passed away within three hours. My sister was changed after that. She is remarried to a great guy, Gary, but is estranged from our family. Her son works with me, so I am able to keep informed about how she is doing. I'm not her caregiver, but when my sister needed help, I was there. And if she needed help today, I would be there as I have always been, and she knows it.

As all this was occurring, I focused on the business. My dad's attention to detail was not there, and he was the world's worst salesman. He ran a printing business, but would never check to see how things went after the job: Did I make money or lose money on this job?

That's how the business got into so much trouble.

When I decided to stay and help rather than let my dad go bankrupt again, he told me, *"You're going to sell."*

That wasn't who I was. *"I don't like people,"* I said. *"I don't want to sell."* I was a 19 year old kid, barely shaving, with no formal sales training. I figured I was doomed to fail.

But I went out to sell. I knocked on doors and talked to people. Fortunately, my first customer took to me like a mother. She gave me the opportunity to quote a job and tried me out.

It was a small job, but I stayed up half the night to get it done and delivered it the next day. That was the beginning of a good relationship. Within six months, she was sending me $20,000 a month of business. The year before, my dad did a grand total of $80,000 in sales for the year.

My dad's right-hand guy was a man named Don Morlock. He was extremely good at what he did and he taught me everything about the shop and how a printing manufacturing business worked. He was a tough nut. I was the boss's son and he wanted to break me.

Don taught me everything about the operations—from wrapping a package to running a folder and running a press. He made my life miserable.

I would wrap 20 packages and Don would break them open and tell me they weren't wrapped tightly enough. I would do it over and over until Don felt they were good enough. To this day, I still wrap the tightest Christmas packages you've ever seen.

Don drove me. Ultimately, it made me the best at what I was doing. I realized that because of the way he taught me, I accomplished things I would otherwise not have been able to do. I always had the work ethic; I just didn't have the knowledge. Don coached me through it and is still with me today. He is 77 years old. I love that man!

When I was 19, I realized my dad was going bankrupt a second time. With the help of my mentors, Stanley Yulish, who was my dad's lawyer and a minority partner in his business, and a gentleman named Art Harad, I learned how to do my first turnaround. Because of that, I was able to take care of my mom and dad until they passed away. That's just the way things had to be.

"Whatever affects one directly, affects all indirectly. I can never be what I ought to be until you are what you ought to be. This is the interrelated structure of reality."

— Martin Luther King, Jr.

1937
Paternal
Grandparents,
Florence and Thomas

1941
Mom and Dad
on their honeymoon

June 20, 1948

My dad, 26 years old

My mom, 24 years old

June 20, 1944

My dad balancing my cousin Judy

My parents. Married May 3, 1941. It lasted
62 years. Dad passed away April 10, 2004
Mom passed away August 4, 2006.

*My brother Tom
(14 years old),
My sister Paula Ann
(7 years old),
and me (5 years old*

*High school
graduation, 1968
"I really had black
hair!"*

Linda and I, 20, and married.

My mom on my 30th birthday.

High school graduation, 1968.
My best childhood friend Tommy.
He passed away a year later.

JUN • 68

High school graduation, 1968. Me with my parents.

Linda and I on our wedding day, June 27, 1970.
43 years and going strong! Thank God.

Mom and Dad's 50th anniversary, 1992

At work at 25 years old. I'm starting to look old.

The reason for this photo is when I say I was in the best shape of mylife, I was in the best shape of my life, at age 57. God had a different plan for me.

I set a senior masters state record at age 51 with a 465-pound deadlift.

10-18-12

Dear One Sight,

Thank you for checking my eyes and for helping me pick the right pair of glasses so I cans see the board better. And you all are the best Eye Sight people ever. Thank you very much!

Love,

Markeya

.P.S.
you are the best.

One of the hundreds of letters Linda and I received from the 12,000 children that had free eye exams an free designer glasses through the OneSight Cleveland program, sponsored by The Luxottica Foundation.

Life is good!
Still madly in love

My daughter Alica's wedding, 2006.

*Loving the manufacturing/printing industry.
One of the first 10 color Heidelberg Presses in
the USA, and the first in Ohio when it was
purchased.*

Chapter 6

Don't Let Anyone Tell You What You Can't Do

"The ultimate measure of a man is not where he stands in moments of comfort and convenience, but where he stands at times of challenge and controversy."

— Martin Luther King, Jr.

No one just drops $30,000 into your lap—especially not in the 1970s, when it was worth much more than it is today. But that's exactly what Ralph Schlag did. He took a chance on me, and that made all the difference in the world.

In 1975, when I was 25 years old, I moved the business from the fifth floor of a building in downtown Cleveland to Chagrin Falls. The downtown facility wasn't meeting our needs anymore. Besides, it was an old building and had bad karma.

A local businessman, Dave Kobick, was selling a printing press in a building in Chagrin Falls. We couldn't afford a new press so I went to talk to him.

I said to Dave, *"Look you've got a press you're not running. I need a press but can't afford to buy one. Let's make a deal."*

I offered him a deal where I would pay him for every 1,000 impressions on the press to cover the rent for the space and use of the press. After 40 hours of running the press, he would get the price he wanted for rent. If we ran the press for two shifts, he'd get double the rent.

Within six months, we had so much business we were running the press 40 hours a week. Within 12 months, we were running it for two shifts—80 hours a week. By 1976, I was at the point where we needed to run the press for three shifts.

I realized that I needed more space, so I went back to Dave and made him a new offer—let's merge businesses.

Dave wasn't interested, so we moved yet again, this time to a building I bought in Bedford. The seller loaned me the money for the down payment because I couldn't get any bank to extend me a mortgage without it.

I also needed a press, so I went to every bank in Cuyahoga County and was turned down. Each told me the same thing: *"Come back when you have some assets and we can talk about loaning you money."*

Then I found out who was in charge of commercial loans at Cleveland Trust.

At the time, Cleveland Trust was one of the biggest banks around, and it was my last resort. My expectation was that it wouldn't even consider giving me a loan. That's why it wasn't on the top of my list. I'd started with smaller, community banks, but that didn't fly.

I went to see Ralph Schlag and told him my story.

He listened intently.

Then Ralph surprised me. He said, *"I'm going to make this loan. This is what we are supposed to do. These are the loans I should be making. You have a vision and I believe you are going to be successful."*

Ralph was the first banker who ever believed in me. Everyone was telling me *"No."* I'd heard *"No"* so many times. Hearing Ralph say *"Yes"* blew me away. I wondered, *"Is this guy playing with a full deck?"* But Ralph is the one who made it happen. He did it.

Then he said to me, "If you do what you say you're going to do, in six months, you'll be back needing operating capital."

I was 25 years old and I thought I knew it all. I told Ralph, *"This is all I need."*

True to Ralph's advice, six months later I was out of cash. I went back to see him, but he was no longer at Cleveland Trust. It took three days of begging his former secretary to get her to tell me where he went. He had moved to Midwest Bank, a small community bank. I sought him out there.

Ralph had expected to hear from me.

"You're out of money, right?" He said.

Sheepishly, I admitted Ralph had been right.

But rather than gloat, he helped me set up a new loan with Midwest Bank that paid off Cleveland Trust and gave me a line of credit for the business.

I never missed a loan payment.

Ralph took a chance on me, so it was my obligation to take care of it. With his help on the financial side and the help of my mentors, I was finally on my way.

Stanley Yulish was instrumental in this process. He had helped my dad buy the business's assets out of bankruptcy and start over. When I met him, I just thought of him as my father's lawyer. He would come to the shop and I'd be working there, so over time I got to know him very well.

Early in my career I didn't know what a mentor was. It was a word I had never heard. Stanley is the person who guided me through that first reorganization, when I was just 19. He helped with the cash flow. He helped us pay down our debt. And he helped us set up credit relationships.

Art Harad, another of my mentors, was a businessman who had gone bankrupt. He explained to me that bankruptcy was just a way of making a mistake; that you could start over with a new company, which I never thought you could do. I thought that if you were once bankrupt, you'd always be bankrupt—once a bust, always a bust.

Whether it is smarts or wisdom, our parents have a lot more than we think they had. Compassion and character—those are two traits I inherited from my mom and dad. Our entire gene pool was blue collar. As far as smarts and business acumen, that came from Stanley and Art. They gave me an education I couldn't buy.

Linda and I were married in 1970; we were both 20 years old. We had our first child, Dena, in 1972. Our second child, Theresa Rose, was born prematurely in 1973, and died after living only 36 hours. Our son, Wally, was born in 1975. And our youngest, Alicia, was born in 1978. By that time, Linda had been pregnant, healing or delivering virtually nonstop for six years. Enough was enough, and we were grateful.

In 1978, Linda's father died. He had been diagnosed with cancer six months before. I took him to God-forsaken mountains in Mexico and helped him get laetrile injections, which was not available in the US. It was his only hope, but it didn't work. That same year, my brother Tom was indicted for aggravated murder. He was put on trial and convicted.

This was an difficult time in my life, dealing with my brother, the business and everything going on. For many years, Linda felt I had abandoned her. In retrospect, I understand why she felt I had abandoned her and the kids. I never clued her in on what I was dealing with or how much work needed to be done.

When my father was having a hard time, he'd come home every night and dump it on my mother. She could never handle the pressure.

I swore I'd never do to Linda, that she would never have to go through that.

What happened was that Linda thought I abandoned her because I took care of everything. I didn't let her know what I was doing and how much of a toll it was taking on me.

Maybe today one could say that was the wrong thing to do, but I think if I had dumped my issues on her while she was pregnant, while raising three small kids and while helping her dying father, it would have pushed her over the edge. In my mind, it was not a good idea to share all of my issues and problems with her. There is a limit to what you can throw at someone, and I thought I was doing the right thing.

So, I never brought the problems home. Since Linda didn't know, her opinion was that I was working so much because I liked to work hard. While work is what I have to do, the level of work I was handling was solely because I had to take care of my parents and my family. It was a long time before I realized how deeply she harbored those feelings. I'd hoped there would be a time, an aha moment, when she would get it, but she couldn't get there.

"My father worked in a factory, but he was home at a certain time every day," Linda says. *"I expected my husband to be the same way—to be home and to help with the kids and around the house. That's not who Ken was. It took many years to reconcile that. We even went to counseling."*

"Ken never quite understood that, Linda says. *"My happiness was having him home with me. I didn't care about the big house. I wanted him there for me and the kids—to be a husband and father. It was hard keeping a family together when he wasn't home a lot."*

That same year, 1978, I invested in a disco. It was a bad deal, and Linda told me I could not do it. Well, I did it anyway. It turned out that Linda was right. The man I loaned the money to was stealing; the other owner was a cocaine addict. My $30,000 was at severe risk of vanishing. So I worked it into my schedule to go to the disco on Friday and Saturday nights to figure out what to do to make it operate and turn a profit. After one weekend, I knew I was in over my head!

To set things straight, I reached out to the owner of a well-known, popular Cleveland bar called The Agora, Hank LoConti, a legend in rock n' roll. LoConti and his club were nationally recognized for giving exposure to numerous bands early in their careers, such as Bruce Springsteen, ZZ Top, Grand Funk Railroad, and The Raspberries. He had been cited by the fire department for overcrowding, which was big news at the time. But to me, that made it look like he really knew what he was doing—packing the house. I didn't get to speak to Hank, instead, I was routed to his nephew, Joe, the club's lawyer.

To this day, Joe LoConti still doesn't know why he took the call or why he agreed to have lunch with me to talk about my club. I laid out my struggles with operating the bar. We worked out a deal—I handed total operations of the club over to him and I would get my original investment back someday. I didn't want any interest or percentages. I just wanted my $30,000 back. It worked out and, for two or three years, all was well.

Then we turned it into a comedy club.

The club was housed in half of a former roller rink. The local Social Security office was in the other half of the building. We opened on a Saturday night with Jackie Vernon as the headliner. That next Sunday night, there was an electrical fire in the sound booth.

Sprinklers had been installed throughout the building. But the Social Security office side had a drop ceiling and the government never dropped their sprinklers down below the new ceilings.

Our sprinklers went off and the club was fine. But the Social Security office in the other half of the building continued to burn. When the heat got to a certain point, the drop ceiling collapsed. That set off all the sprinklers in the building. They ran all night and into the next morning.

The first person that walked into the Social Security office on Monday morning found water pouring out from under the doors. The water destroyed our space, too.

The government thought that because my brother, Tom, had previously been indicted on RICO charges and was allegedly involved in organized crime, this was an overt action against the government. They held up the insurance proceeds for months and months, and we went out of business.

Later, the fire department said there was no appearance of arson, and that it wasn't an action against the government. Truly, in this case, shit just happened. It was the federal government that was negligent for not moving the sprinklers when they put the dropped ceiling in the Social Security office. If the sprinklers had been properly moved below the ceiling, there would have been almost no damage to either side of the building.

It's amazing that people often tell you what you can't do rather than what you can. I've learned over the years that it's more important to believe in your own abilities than to worry about what other people say. Don't let anyone tell you what you can't do. I found that out the hard way—through trial and error.

One part of my gift is that in business I am the calm in the storm (most of the time). I can't dance or sing or play a musical instrument, but I am blessed with a sense of calm and an ability to put organization into chaos. It's an innate skill, part of my personality. At times, I may do things to help others when it makes no sense to do so.

Maybe I lack a little bit of common sense at those times, but I believe that to the extent you can do something, you do it. Only with my cardiac arrest, and all of the following events, did I get frustrated. If something isn't right, I push until I find the right path. I run multiple businesses at the same time; I deal with employees, clients and vendors. It's just what I do. Nobody asks me, people seem to just expect me to take care of things; it's been that way my whole life. And I am OK with that. If I can, I do.

Until the late 1970s, I didn't necessarily think of myself as a successful businessman. The turning point was one day when I wanted to buy something, a piece of equipment for the shop. I looked at my bank statement and realized I was doing pretty well. Then I talked with a banker about a loan and he said, *"No problem."*

I had come a long way from Ralph and all the bankers before him. I realized I had made it from point A to point B. So I cashed a check for $100 and put the cash in my pocket. Then I thought, *"This is pretty good!"* I've always provided for others, but now I had something extra for myself.

On a Saturday, I went to Sears to buy a grass catcher for my lawn mower. Then I saw these moon shoes with crepe soles about an inch and a half thick. They were brown with suede and looked really comfortable.

Then the responsible side of me kicked in.

"Do I really need this?" I thought. *"No,"* I told myself. *"But I can afford it!"*

That was the first thing I did for myself, the first thing I bought just for me. I kept those shoes for more than 25 years. I had provided for everyone else and now I was able to buy something I didn't need. I've never looked back.

I often speak to kids about being successful. I can sum it up pretty succinctly: Have you ever had a piggy bank?

If you put a dime in your piggy bank every day, after 1,000 days, there will be 1,000 dimes. That's $100.

But if you put nothing into that piggy bank, in 1,000 days, you will still have nothing. So what makes you think you have anything coming to you if you don't do it yourself?

Your brain is the same way, I tell them. Learn as much as you can. Fill your brain until it overflows. Then, years from now, when you need it, you'll be happy you have it. And it will take you through the rest of your life.

No matter how much you fill your brain, this is how most of us live—by our opinions. It's not necessarily guided by facts. Rather, our opinions often are formed by what somebody may have told us. It could be totally wrong. Somebody may have heard from somebody, six degrees of a story, and it completely changes.

As I have previously mentioned, this concept has been a guiding principle in my life. In business meetings, tell me what you know, not what you think. If we have a problem, we have to talk about what we know. Solving a problem is not just thinking I know the answer. It's quite simple: Do you know the answer or don't you?

If you don't know, let's go around the room and find someone who does. And if no one in the room knows, let's think about a way to approach this. If you work on the basis of fact and strive for knowledge instead of guessing at the answer—and a lot of thinking is really guessing—then we'll all be a lot better off.

Thinking ahead, being prepared and planning for the future can make all the difference in your life. Keeping my nose to the grindstone has helped me succeed. But being a millionaire today is not like it was in times past. It's not like it was in the 1950s.

I shouldn't minimize it; my first million was still a million. It was the early 1980s, I was in my early 30s, when I realized that my net worth was $1 million. I realized that, with real estate and equipment, I had the ability to leverage those assets to do more.

But that realization was anti-climactic. Having achieved that level of success did not give me a sense of security, there was no sense of: *"I have arrived! I can take it easy!"* No, the demands on me were too great to kick back and feel secure. If I had a life of just me, my wife and kids, I would have been more liquid and might have enjoyed some measure of security.

But I had my parents and a family that needed help. As hard as I worked, I had to continue to keep the cash flowing. I needed more to get through every week and month. In fact, I sometimes borrowed money just to meet the needs of others.

It was never, *"Can you do this?"* or, *"Can you do that?"* It was always, *"I need this."* or, *"I need that."*

If I am going to do something for somebody, I don't think about whether or not I am going to be repaid. I do it because it's the right thing to do. This sense of giving comes from my mom. She never expected anything in return.

If you truly are working for the greater good of others, like a wife and family, the journey is far better than if you're just doing it for yourself. Doing it for yourself becomes very selfish and doesn't allow you to work toward the goal. Working every day to provide and create a future is hard work—especially when others are saying it can't be done.

I didn't drink. I didn't go to college. I worked hard. And there was no way I was going to take a chance to get drunk and miss the bell. In my position, given the consequences, I couldn't fail. I had to work, work and work even harder. That was the key to becoming successful.

When I was 19 or 20, $100,000 a year was like a $1 million. I couldn't even imagine it. It was way beyond my thought process that it could ever exist. As a businessman, I learned that it takes money to make money. And I learned that you can't let anyone tell you what you can or can't do.

In order to make big money, you have to work harder than you ever imagined. You can make a living working 40 hours a week. But you can't work 40 hours a week and be totally secure. You'll have to work harder if you want to make a lot of money. And you'll have to ignore all of those around you that say you can't do it.

"So faith by itself, if it has no works, is dead."
— James 2:17

Chapter 7

Getting in the Box

*"A man does what he must—in spite of personal consequences,
in spite of obstacles and dangers, and pressures—and that is the
basis of all human morality."*

— John F. Kennedy

In this world, in my opinion, there are only two kinds of
people: Those inside the box with connections, money and
access. And then there are the rest of us.

My education in this began when I started to sell. Selling was
outside my comfort zone. I was meeting and talking to new people,
so I watched how they behaved. I was trying to fast-forward my
maturity level enough to be taken seriously. That was a challenge.

Sales, as I've learned over the years, is all about relationships.
And when you are 19 or 20 years old, you don't have a lot in
common with the people you are speaking with. You listen to
your parents. When I was that age, I was in the transition of

leaving home, getting married and getting out into the world of other adults who were making a living.

My first real opportunity to develop a true sales relationship came with a woman named Millie Herenko, a new client I had called on.

Millie more or less mothered me. I was honest and told her that I was new to sales. *"I know what I'm doing,"* I had said. *"It's just that I'm not that good at selling it."*

She took me under her wing.

Millie took great satisfaction in giving me some work and then some more. We delivered on what she needed. I met the challenges and she continued to support my efforts. I was grateful for that. The few years that I worked with her helped me hone my sales skills and understand how I needed to communicate in order to be successful.

Millie had four sons of her own. One was about my age. I think she saw in me what she probably saw in her kids and felt, *"Gee, if my kid was out there, I would hope somebody would help him."*

I feel that Millie gave me the opportunity—more from a maternal instinct rather than her business instincts. But at least she gave me a chance. To this day, I'm extremely grateful.

At some point in life, and in business, someone has to give you a break. That philosophy has followed me through my entire life. And that is the moment when you get in the box. Whether or not you are prepared to get in it is purely up to each of you.

I talk to kids about this idea all the time.

I ask them to visualize a box.

If they are outside the box and not ready to get into it when they get a chance, then shame on them, because, I tell them, they won't get many chances.

We go to school to learn; what we really learn there are facts. Learning about life is what happens every day, basically any hour of the day, whenever we are awake. I tell kids they have to seize that opportunity and recognize that life is not about playing basketball or video games. It's about something much more important.

Learning is about recognizing what others do for a living, looking to people you respect and admire, and trying to copy that. It's about spending time with them and listening when they talk, because that's how we pick up knowledge about the world.

When we get the opportunity to get into the box, we have to be ready. We have to understand our surroundings and be book smart.

I explain that once they get out of high school, they have to be looking for opportunities. Those who are fortunate enough to go to college have a tremendous number of role models to spend time with and aspire to be like—professors, administrators, older classmates, etc. This time in their life is an opportunity to work toward the future.

Again, I tell them, whether they go to college or not, these are the most important years of their lives. No one ever gets these years back. Every day, the bell is rung and no one can go back to re-ring yesterday's bell. You ring today's bell, then tomorrow's, and then the next day's. You can't go back; there are no do-overs. TPITP—the past is the past.

One day, I spoke to my grandson's class. Each student gets to invite someone in his or her family to come in to talk about what he or she does, and my grandson asked me. I talked with the kids about the box and my *"Lanci Logic Line of Life."*

I drew a line on the chalkboard and put a zero at the far left of the line. Then I put an 85 at the far right of the line. Between, starting on the left, I put a 6, 12, 18, 24, 30, 40, 50, and 60, with each number representing an age of their lives. Then you identify where you are at that time on the line.

For that class of sixth-graders, I put a mark at 12. I showed them were I was—60. I said that their parents were probably in the 30s or early 40s.

"What bothers you kids about us adults," I explained, *"is that you think we don't understand what you are going through, that we don't have any idea. I'm here to tell you that we do. In order to get to 30 or 40 or 60 on the line, we started over on the left, at zero. We know exactly what you are going through because we already went through it."*

Then I gave them a news flash; the things that we adults did in our youth that were wrong or hurtful to do, we try to stop kids from doing. We have learned since that they were wrong or hurtful. And we do that because we love them. *"If we didn't' care, we would just let you run wild and get into trouble."*

"Between this number," I said as I pointed to 12, *"and 18 is a significant time in your life, because at 18 you are on your own. You join the ranks of the adults. That means you are responsible for 100 percent of what you do. What you need to understand is that to make it to 18, you need to know as much as you can to prevent yourselves from ending up in trouble."*

With some inner-city kids, the key message is that they do have a choice. I tell them the brutal truth: If they choose not to listen to the adults around them, there is a good chance that by the time they turn 21, they will be state-raised or dead.

"It's your choice," I say. *"And choose wisely."*

"Adults are not talking down to kids when we say things like this. We are talking to you about what we've seen and what we've been through and are trying to point out what could happen to you. It is easy to think that this stuff won't happen to you, but it can and does. It happened to me. So we are trying to help because we love you and want good things for you."

"Understand that from now on," I explain, *"if you see a line, it is no longer just a line. It is how you want to live the rest of your life."*

"It is a path to guide your life in the direction you want to go."

Two weeks after my visit with his class, my grandson brought an envelope to our Sunday dinner. It was filled with letters from the kids in his class. I was blown away at the level of comprehension that these kids took away from my talk. They said, *"I will never look at a line the same way again,"* and *"Wow, thank you for telling me about the box."* This stuff didn't go over their heads. They got it.

In urban communities, the attitude of inner-city kids and young adults is often: *"I'm not going to conform to what The Man wants me to do."*

I tell them you don't have to conform. But if you don't, you are not going to get anywhere. You are either in or out of the box, that's your choice. You cannot change the box.

WORKING FOR THE GREATER GOOD OF ALL ... REALLY

Think about it. News anchors don't have nose rings. Police officers, doctors and businesspeople don't wear their pants halfway off their asses. If you want to be successful, you have to learn to do things the right and acceptable way.

That said, what you do in your private time with your life is your business. We all understand that. But you don't get a pass to be the goof you may have been in your youth. It doesn't work that way. You don't get in the box during the day and get out of it on your way home. Getting in the box is a challenge. Staying in it is harder.

At some point, each of us has to make a life choice. If you get into the box, you are in the box every day, 24 hours a day. When you decide you have either made enough money or no longer need to conform, then you can get out of the box and out of the game. At that point, you can do anything you want your own way, as long as it doesn't impact others' rights and safety.

Once I realized the big difference in the opportunities available to me while inside the box versus those outside of it, there wasn't anything I wouldn't do to strengthen my position and stay inside it. I worked hard to never, ever, reach even the edge of the box. And to a fault, I labored.

That extends to how I compose myself, quiet and thoughtful— as well as how I dress—professionally.

"People who don't know Ken think he's a little intimidating," says Linda. *"I think it's because of the way he carries himself. Once people sit down and talk to him, they know what he's like. He's honest. He's straightforward. But he's not intimidating."*

To this day, I still try to acquire as much knowledge as possible from the people in the box who are smarter than me.

And believe me, over the years, there have been a lot of them. There is a never-ending supply of people smarter than I am, so I open my mind, set my ego aside, listen and learn.

I also learned that there is nothing wrong with saying, *"I don't know that. I don't know how to do that. Can you help me?"*

Admitting you don't know something or asking for help are not weaknesses. It's only a sign of weakness if you've already been told the same thing multiple times and failed to act on it.

The simple truth is that all of us have questions—we can't be experts on everything. You must realize that as we grow, we develop our skills or focus on an occupation where we want to excel. But keep in mind, just because you're 10 years into your career doesn't mean you're qualified to be an expert heart surgeon, a master plumber or a skilled electrician. Whatever it is you choose to focus on, you must keep practicing, learning and working to fine-tune your skills. This is a daily challenge and underscores the importance of continuous learning.

It doesn't matter what you choose as your focus—every job in every sector is critical to the larger picture in society. Over the years, I've heard people say, *"Wow. I'm just a teacher. Look at that rocket scientist. Boy, I'd like to be a rocket scientist."*

My reply is always the same: *"Well, he may be a good rocket scientist, but he wouldn't be able to teach the way you do—to have the patience, talent and the professional skill set you have. That's what you have developed. That's what you do. And it's important, too."*

Your life should never be focused on another person's ability to do something that you can't. Rather, it should be about the choices you can make. Isn't that what life is really all about— making choices? I tell kids, *"If you choose a career that you enjoy, you'll never work a day in your life."* And I emphasis the point that it is very important to make real choices instead of just letting life take you where it wishes. When that happens, you end up someplace random, and you'll never be happy.

One of the biggest differences between people inside the box and those outside of it is their use of language. Being an articulate speaker is important. Word choices when you speak and write can limit your opportunities and prevent you from reaching your full potential. Words and phrases such as *"ya know," "ummm," "like," "OK"* or *"you follow me"* are not necessary in an intelligent conversation. They're used to fill space, to keep hearing ourselves speak. Professional talk is more structured, and those people inside the box understand this. They learn how to pause and let the other people in a conversation speak instead of trying to fill space.

Here's an example.

If one of your friends stopped by and asked if you wanted to do something, they might say, *"Hey, would you like, ya know, want to go, umm, to a movie?"*

How does that sound?

It sounds like that person isn't sure of him or herself or what he or she wants to do. When you're inside the box, you wouldn't approach it this way. Instead, the question would be direct, *"Would you like to go see a movie?"*

It's short, to the point and there's no hesitation.

While it sounds trite, I learned this hard lesson when I was 23 years old. A good friend, Kenny Schmidt, and I were talking one evening and he finally said, *"Ken, stop talking in the middle of a sentence. You are driving me nuts. Every other word out of your mouth is 'ya know.'"*

At first, I was a bit offended. I replied, *"I don't think so."*

"OK," Kenny said. *"Why don't you start talking and I will raise my hand every time you say it."*

So I stated talking, and within a few seconds, Kenny was waving his hand. I kept talking. The more I talked, the more he waved. Soon, he was waving his hand so frequently that he looked like Princess Diana riding in a motorcade.

"OK. OK. OK," I said. *"I get your point."*

Everything Kenny said was true. It was an aha moment, and I recognized my speech needed to be more professional. Kenny's willingness to correct me for my own good became a game-changer. I began focusing on how inadequate my vocabulary was and worked hard to break my bad habits. I started paying more attention to how other people spoke— especially those inside the box, people who didn't use what I like to call *"interrupters."*

Try this exercise the next time you are either in a meeting or out and about in public: Listen to the people in the box. Listen to how they speak. I'm not talking about the ones who were born in the box—people who were born into privilege. Rather, listen to the ones who have worked hard to get there. You'll find that they have developed very good habits in how they speak, and people pay attention to them when they're talking.

If you truly care about someone, then it's your responsibility to tell him or her if he or she uses the kind of words one shouldn't. It's important for you to help people succeed by pointing out that their language may be limiting them and their ability to stretch themselves further. While they may be a little offended at first, they'll eventually get over it. This is the right thing to do, and you can be sure that if the person you say it to trusts and respects you, then he or she will give what you say some deeper thought later.

To this day, I am very grateful for the advice Kenny provided. He cared about me enough to tell me the truth. I often tell my family, friends and other children the story about how I lost those words I didn't need to be saying. And the payoff for me was feeling more secure and confident when I spoke to people. In fact, I felt more comfortable working inside the box than I ever had before.

A major turning point in my life as I tried to get into that box was when I was 26 years old. I drove out to the Coliseum in Richfield, Ohio, which at the time was the new arena where the Cleveland Cavaliers and the Cleveland Crusaders hockey club were going to play.

Pro sports teams do a lot of printing—posters, programs, signs and such—so I drove out there to make a sales call. I had learned who was in charge of marketing and finally was able to get an appointment to see him.

I pitched him and he pitched me.

"We like to do business with people who like to do business with us," he said.

I thought to myself, 'Sure I can buy some tickets.'

He said, *"We have loges."*

"What's a loge?" I asked.

He eyeballed me for a moment, and then we got into an elevator and went up one level from the meeting room. We walked down the hallway and into a living room. At the far end of the room was a window with a view of the arena in front of us.

"Wow!" I said. *"This is cool."*

The man smiled. *"You can have one of these if you sign a contract with us,"* he said.

"I'll tell you what," I replied. *"Why don't you sign a contract with me and give me all your printing?"*

"A loge is $10,000 down and $10,000 a year for 10 years," he explained.

I was taken aback, but didn't show it. I had paid only $30,000 for my house five years earlier. This was a very large commitment. I gathered myself and asked, *"How much printing do you have?"*

"Between the Cavaliers and the Crusaders, as well as special events, about $200,000 a year," he said.

"OK," I exclaimed. *"Then I am your only printer and I can share my tickets with clients."*

We agreed to the deal on the spot. That's the truest definition of a risk-taker; no risk, no reward.

I had to take a second mortgage on my house for the down payment, but this was a big-league decision. To put things in perspective, Linda and I were married. We had two children. And neither of us had ever seen a professional basketball game. That I took a second mortgage on our house didn't sit too well with her. But it was the right decision at the right time.

For the first two years, I took family and clients. Eventually, I just sent clients. When I consummated the deal, my business was generating about $1 million a year. Three to four years later, we were doing about $3 million in annual sales. This deal was the moment when I realized that the opportunity to get into the box was a real one.

Another person who helped me bridge the gap from outside the box to inside it was Tony Fatica, owner of then Ad-man Graphics (today, AMG Advertising and Public Relations). Tony and I spoke openly about my shortcomings—how I hadn't gone to college and what I didn't learn because of it. I asked Tony to help me improve my language.

What Tony would do is stop me when I was talking and rephrase my sentences. He did it thoughtfully and without embarrassing me. Usually, it was in his office.

As Tony and I spoke, if I would say something wrong, he would stop and correct me. I was very grateful for the opportunity to have him to correct my speech, and Tony's help provided another step forward in getting into the box.

Things were moving along nicely at this point of my career. Because of the attention I was giving to my self-improvement, I was now able to talk the talk. I owned a loge at the Coliseum. I was dealing at the right level with people who could and were willing to help me. You could say I forced myself into the box through a baptism by fire. I essentially did what I had to do, and I've never looked back.

By the time I was 35 years old I had developed several new skills and felt a lot more capable than I had just a few years earlier. Sometimes, when I met new people, they would ask, *"Where did you go to school?"*

I would tell them the name of my high school.

"No," they'd say. *"Where did you go to college?"*

I enjoyed hearing that question because it provided validation of my hard work. The truth is, I never had the same opportunity as others who were able to go to college for four years, focus on polishing themselves, and then go out into the world to build a career. It may have taken me a little longer to get polished, but I put my mind to it and still was successful. In some ways, however, at age 35 I was far ahead of those who were just coming out of school at 22 or 23 years old. My children were born. I had a family. And I already had a successful business. My life plan had already exceeded my expectations.

One of my greatest strengths is ignorance. That may sound odd, but not knowing things or not thinking that I couldn't do whatever it was I was trying to do, never stood in the way of trying. When dealing with my dad's bankrupt company, I wasn't upset, nervous or intimated because I didn't know I was supposed to be. I wasn't afraid of any of it. I just attacked the problem.

My father, on the other hand, refused to face problems. He would throw things into the wastebasket or in a drawer. He was reactionary and would wait until something happened before he faced it. He rarely attacked a problem until it reached the point where something had to be done. Once I managed the business through its turnaround, I began to realize the difference. I started to understand that in a normal business situation, you plan. Standing still and waiting for something to happen doesn't work. You are either in or you're out.

At my core I am an entrepreneur. Entrepreneurs learn how to take nothing and make it into something. Then, when they have something, they grow it, figure out how to manage it, finance it, hire employees and keep them happy, and yes, work ungodly hours.

I am not a caretaker. That's a job best left for professional managers. I've realized that I have to be an innovator. Too many times I have watched organizations that are led by caretakers fail to advance. Caretakers do continue to do things that have always been done, and they do not think differently or find new ways to do old things. That's the current definition of most politicians.

In today's fast-paced world, building a successful business means creating something that can operate as efficiently without you as it does with you. Of course, there are decisions that you, as the CEO, will need to make because it's your money. But there are also decisions that you must allow others to make because you've hired them to do so. You need to learn to trust their judgment. With my personal management team, I've become very comfortable that their experience and knowledge is just what's needed to move our organization ahead.

The older I get, the better I've become at identifying trends, problems and situations—long before they blow up. Experience does that for you. I've seen the pitfalls and land mines that await any business, and I have learned that the difference between being smart and dumb is being able to learn from previous mistakes you've made.

Part of what makes America great is our ability to come together in times of crisis, just like we did after September 11, 2001, and at other times during our nation's history. It's something that's unique. But we are losing the war of smarts, which is sure to have severe negative consequences.

The truth is that we need to expect more out of each other, just like we do in the business world. We need to expect more out of our fellow countrymen, more from our states, counties, towns and townships. And we need to expect more out of our elected leaders at all levels. If we want to continue to push things forward, we need to start helping each other improve— bring each of us into the box. We have an obligation to each other to do more.

"I look forward to an America which commands respect throughout the world, not only for its strength but for its civilization as well. And I look forward to a world which will be safe not only for democracy and diversity but also for personal distinction."

— John F. Kennedy

Chapter 8

Fifty-Eight Parades

"Trust in the Lord with all your heart, and lean not on your own understanding; In all your ways acknowledge Him. And he shall direct your paths."

— Proverbs 3:5,6

If Cuyahoga County had been for sale, I'd have bought it. And then I would have fixed it. After all, that's what I do for businesses: I turn them around.

Running for county executive in 2010 was not really my decision. Issue 6 changed the form of county government from three commissioners to one county executive and a council. It was a new charter, the startup of a new government and merged different offices within the county as part of an effort to change the culture. The job was everything I'd done successfully over the past 30 years and required a skill set that could not have been more personally tailored for someone like me.

Still, when I thought about it, I had doubts.

"I'm not a politician, forget about it," was the conversation I had with myself over and over.

Then, one morning, I woke up and thought that perhaps this was what I was supposed to do. If I was alive in order to accomplish something specific, surely it wasn't just to run my business.

I made my decision; I was going to run for office. Some friends kept asking me why I was doing it. Why not just go to the beach and relax?

I explained that I believed it was the right thing for me to do to help my community, and I was worried that if I went to the beach, laid back and relaxed in my chair, then that would be it. I would end up standing in front of God, and He would say, *"Ken, that's not what I wanted you to do. You totally blew it. Go to the end of the line!"*

Luckily, Linda was supportive when I told her I was going to run. She was a real trooper; she really was, especially after we started campaigning. And it didn't take long for her to become my secret weapon.

Linda organized groups, campaigned and knocked on doors—a lot of them. She was very disappointed when I lost. I felt bad for her, as well as the workers who supported me, after the results came in. I am not one of those people who become emotional after something happens. To me, losing the election was just stuff. I was more disappointed for my family and my supporters because of all the hard work they had done.

Running for office was the right thing for me to do. I knew that when I woke up the next morning. There was no more money to spend and no more meetings to hold. During the 10 months of my campaign, I had more than 1,000 meetings and events. And during that time, I put it all out there. The outcome was what it was, and there was a reason why I didn't win.

There are 58 heads of cities and townships in Cuyahoga County. I spoke to about 30 of them during my campaign. The others refused to meet me because they were staunch Democrats and I ran for office as an Independent. I spoke to a lot of businesspeople, too. They had no problem fitting me in and talking to me. They were always very gracious and nice.

None of the other candidates held as many meetings as I did. I am certain of that. In fact, I can say with certainty that I knew more about the inner workings of Cuyahoga County's government structure at that time than the man who won the election.

One of the things I learned during my campaign was that politicians don't often run for a job, they run for a position. And most don't have the right experience for the job they're seeking. Basically, they just run for a position and try to win. Combined, I don't think the other candidates had more than a half of the county meetings I had — and there were half a dozen candidates! None of them spent time looking into the business of the county like I did. And even if they had, I don't think they would have known what to look for.

As part of my due diligence, I spoke with directors at more than 60 county agencies. Most of them seemed surprised that I wanted to meet with them, but they were gracious and happy to talk to someone who was genuinely interested in what was working and what wasn't working at their agency.

In each of these meetings, I would ask the directors what were their biggest issues. I would ask: *"If you had the ability to fix what's wrong in your department, what would you fix right now?"*

The first response was usually a blank look, but then each of them came up with some good ideas. We discussed how that change would fix the problem and what it would do for the department. These conversations often took up to two hours each, but they resulted in solutions that could be considered. My campaign administrator, Gwen Dillingham, joined me in the meetings and took notes. When we returned to my office, Gwen put the information into a binder for that specific agency.

My plan was straightforward: After I won the election, I would meet each of these directors, one at a time, and remind them of our conversation—the problems and the solutions we discussed. Then I would tell them to implement the solution. This was a totally different approach than any of the other candidates took.

It all goes back to what you can learn in business. If you are going to buy a company, you must make time for due diligence. You collect all the facts; then you verify them. This is how you determine if and how you can fix a company's problems. It provides the necessary transparency to analyze whether a business can be turned around or if it's a lost cause.

One thing I learned during the campaign is that voters really wanted change. There was no doubt about that.

I received 11 percent of the vote—a total of 47,000 people voted for me. That is a lot of people consciously making the decision to choose someone different.

However, 125,000 people voted for an indicted judge just because she was a Democrat—she wouldn't have been able to serve even if she won the election. That was an instance of Democrats purely voting Democrat. The people who voted for me did so because they liked what I had to say and believed I could do what I said I was going to do. More important, they were willing to speak with their vote and say they wanted something completely different.

For a while during the campaign, I had a weekly radio show that lasted two to three hours each Sunday. Each show, I would get around 50 calls. People really liked what I had to say. Some of the people who called in had wrong perceptions or opinions about things because they didn't have all the facts, so I would lay the facts out for them. Afterward, the callers would thank me for clearing things up. It was a very refreshing experience.

I would spend each show answering questions and ensuring that I didn't insult the people who called. I kept a researcher with me at the station, so that if I didn't know the answer to a question right away, by the end of the conversation, I usually had it. Only a few times were we unable to find the answer while we were on the air. In those rare instances, we asked callers if they'd like us to call them back. If they said they yes, we did. Because of this, I never had a caller who said I didn't know what I was talking about.

When it was time to end the show, about two weeks before the last show, I announced on the air that I was leaving. For the next two weeks, a woman kept calling and begging me to keep the show. *"Please, please don't stop,"* she would beg. *"I look forward to hearing you every week."*

People like that made me feel I was making a difference.

During the campaign, one question rose to the forefront of all the others I was asked: *"Why are you doing this? You don't need to do this."*

I would explain my story—the cardiac arrest, my death and the belief that I needed to work for the greater good of all. I talked about my journey of faith, and my belief that if it were meant to happen, I would win. If not, I wouldn't.

One concern I heard from voters was the issue of government corruption. This was the entire reason why Issue 6 and the election came to be—the existing county commissioner system was corrupt. In the time since, two of the largest players in the scandal have been convicted on corruption charges. One was sentenced to 22 years in prison; the other 28 years.

People had reached a point where they were fed up with this kind of unethical behavior from politicians. They were disappointed that the people in charge were not taking care of them as constituents but rather were taking care of themselves. People woke up to realize that long-serving politicians were more self-serving than benevolent.

The people who supported me did so because they felt I was straightforward. Plus, I didn't need the job. I made it very clear that I would not take a paycheck if I was elected. I also financed my own campaign, so I didn't owe anyone anything—especially politically. If I were going to have the job, I would have it for the right reasons. I would be committed to serving the people of Cuyahoga County and working hard to make it a better place to live and work.

After the election, I heard one sentiment several times: *"I would have voted for you, but I figured you didn't have a chance to win because you ran as an Independent. I didn't want to waste my vote."*

That doesn't upset me (it just is what it is). Cuyahoga County is a staunchly Democratic county. Republicans rarely are elected to countywide offices; Independents are nonexistent. Just to demonstrate the point, consider that, in both the 2008 and the 2012 elections, President Barack Obama carried Cuyahoga County with nearly 70 percent of the vote.

Before the campaign, I was never much of a parade guy. During the campaign, however, I participated in more than 50 parades. The only way I was able to accomplish this was divine intervention. It takes a lot of energy to walk a mile or two, wave, shake hands and hand out candy to the kids. When you walk in parades, you must stay upbeat, which required a substantial amount of energy. But you know what? I never got tired.

My first parade was Memorial Day 2010. I hit two parades that day—one in the morning and another in the afternoon. At each parade, we had approximately 50 people walking with us — supporters, family and friends. As part of our parade presence, we also had trucks wrapped with my picture. There was no missing us.

We wrapped my campaign advertisements around seven RTA buses as part of our media buys. Sometimes, one of those buses would join us for the parades. They were dynamite. Linda was shocked when she saw them for the first time. We hadn't discussed buying ads on buses around town, and even though I knew they were coming, I forgot to tell Linda about them. We also had 70 other buses, with side panels, travelling the county.

One day, Linda called me from her car to tell me that a bus pulled up alongside her. When she turned her head to look at it, she was staring at my giant face. It was a bit unnerving.

As we walked along the parade routes, my team and I handed out T-shirts and Tootsie Roll Pops. 2010 was a very hot summer, so we also produced thousands of little handheld fans. We passed those out during the first four weeks.

"Every American ought to have the right to be treated as he would like to be treated, as one would wish to be treated, as one would wish his children to be treated."

— John F. Kennedy

Chapter 9

Broken

"All that is necessary for the triumph of evil is that good men do nothing."

— Edmund Burke

I wasn't always frustrated with banks and Wall Street. In fact, I spent a lot of time building relationships with banks. But today, based on everywhere you turn and everything you read, it seems both the banks and Wall Street have made it more difficult for the middle class and the poor. For me, that's completely unacceptable—especially when everything I do these days has the greater good in mind.

To be fair, no one group is at fault. Everyone is culpable. Each group has played its part because of the way the system has been set up. We are all to blame for this because we have all accepted the decline of the middle class. And we have come to accept an opaque paradigm where it is every man and woman for him or herself. But it never had to reach this level.

Sadly, the banks, Wall Street and our own government did little to stop the escalation. And this is why we eventually reached the economic meltdown of 2008 and have been so slow to recover.

We should have been smarter. We should have seen it was unrealistic. We should have seen the improbability of the situation. It should have been unbelievable. But America wanted more, and everyone saw it exactly the same way – as an opportunity to rise up economically more easily than previous generations had.

So the middle class got hooked. They invested their retirement savings, 401(k) money and disposable income and jumped in with both feet. And it didn't take long – just a few short years – before everything imploded, taking retirement savings and the housing market with it.

I often sit and wonder if we had done things differently, if we had paid more attention, that we could have somehow avoided this mess. But over the years, our government has become much more politicized, and that has made working together for the greater good more difficult.

Compromise wasn't easy years ago, but it also wasn't a dirty word. It wasn't considered treason against your party to make a deal with someone across the aisle because it was in the best interest of the population as a whole. And when compromise happened, people were able to get done what needed to be done.

Instead, many things went unchecked. And in the early part of the 2000s, you didn't need a down payment to buy a house. Heck, you didn't even need a job. So the mortgage and finance companies were more than happy to give people a loan for more money than they could afford, at an unbelievable interest rate. It effectively created deals that people couldn't refuse.

And, because of the increased flow of deals, home prices rose to unrealistic levels. People began to believe their home value would keep going up—forever. It was a cyclical process. As more people bought homes under the belief that it would be an ever-value-increasing asset, a secondary market appeared —refinancing. Suddenly, all equity was being sucked out of real estate at an alarming rate.

In my opinion, this is an even greater disaster because before this time in history, people had always counted on having real estate left to them by previous generations as the legacy of the lifetime work completed by their parents and grandparents. Parents bought within their means, diligently paid off the mortgage notes and left a debt-free home to their children.

While we didn't completely understand what was happening at the time, it's now become crystal clear. Wall Street and investment banks packaged three types of loans: A (very good), B (OK) and C (bad)—and sold them to the world. They were designed to be confusing, spread the risk and, ultimately, were not built for the long term. And when all the money was finally sucked out of the system, the banks saw they were not collecting on their loans, and they said, "This isn't working either."

That was in September 2008, and the world came crashing down. Things haven't been the same since.

It's sad, really. In today's America, we have a dichotomy of values. But we can't have it both ways. At some point, I hope everyone comes to the realization that it isn't about winning or losing. It should be about compromise, working together and moving this great country forward. Otherwise, the middle class and the poor will continue to suffer.

My business, Consolidated Graphics Group, is primarily business-to-business. We experienced our share of ups and downs due to the economy. We do a lot of work for retail companies, so the strength of the market dictates how much money they have to put into play. We haven't seen a significant drop in business over the past decade, but we must fight much harder for everything we get. Margins are smaller and we must work harder and smarter than the competition.

So you can imagine how frustrating it is for me to look around and see what's going on around me. I care about the greater good of all. I care that hard work should translate into opportunities. And opportunities seem fewer and more far between for people in the middle class and the poor. Having grown up the way I did, it causes me pain to watch what's happening—especially since we refuse to learn from the past.

The economic downturn affected me in the sense that I saw more people in need of help. My personal finances are OK. It's just that I have responsibilities for so many other people. It's what I call my "disposable income"—it's the money that allows me to get involved and help others. As things slowed down and cash got tighter, it has been harder for me to do as many things to help others as part of the greater good.

So much of this crisis was preventable. Think about the mortgage fiasco. Even today, five years after the fallout from the problems started, there are still a large number of people who can't make their payments.

They remain in their houses and the process to foreclose takes so long that they could spend a year or two there without making payments. For a lot of people, that would help them get their finances straight. For others, they just remain in the hole they're in because they've opted to spend the money they're saving by not paying a dime on their mortgages.

Once again, in my opinion, we are failing our citizens here. We need to work together to right the situation in order to impact the greater good. Otherwise, abandoned houses will continue go to auction for two-thirds appraised value. Homes will continue to get trashed. People will continue to get displaced. And they will continue to lose more money. In some neighborhoods, there are so many empty homes that I fear they will never recover.

The economic challenges facing Cuyahoga County have been here from the beginning. Over the years, those of us who live here have learned how to do more with less. So when the economy finally turns around the way it eventually will, we'll be in great shape to capitalize on it because we didn't get into that much debt. This is a region where there are still a lot of opportunities because we didn't have that massive economic downturn. There is more than $9 billion of development going on right now, which is great for our future.

My experience running for county executive was the equivalent of stepping behind the curtain and seeing the wizard pull the strings. I was a political outsider trying to make a positive change where I live by getting involved at a higher level. And this is when I fully realized what I had thought for years—that the political process is broken.

My greatest shock when I ran for county executive was learning the depths of inefficiency and abuse that plagued the system. I always thought the role of county government was to provide services for the needy and take care of people who were unable to help themselves.

I learned this view was naïve. There is a broken mentality that has permeated society—the best way to do things is the way they've always been done. As part of my political journey, I visited more than 60 different agencies. I discovered that the goal was not to change or improve things or even to follow best practices. It was simply to fight and maintain the status quo. Few in the county government had the desire or ability to look at the big picture from a business perspective and try to solve the problems. Nobody was interested in trying to implement new or innovative ideas or even to adapt best practices.

I found that there was really no role for somebody like me— an outsider who just wanted to help turn things around. I found that businessmen can't do anything to change government while standing on the outside. And what I realized from having started on the outside to run for political office is that getting into office is the only way you can make a difference in how the system is structured and run. Once I entered the race, people began talking to me. During the campaign I received a lot of attention because there was a possibility of winning and getting into office, and people wanted to hear what I would do if that happened.

My friends watched this experience up close and personal. And what they saw impacted them as much as it did me. "Our community needs more Ken Lancis," says Stuart Muszynski. "Unfortunately, there aren't a lot of them. There aren't a lot of people in the community who will basically see anybody. There are people who are doing things on the surface but not a lot who have the depth of caring and concern and are willing to get their hands dirty, meet with anybody and do anything to improve our community. Those are unique people. And that is Ken.

For someone like me, who desires significant change to help the greater good of all, my experience running for elected office was positive in that it encouraged me to keep trying to make a change. It is why I continue to do what I do now, even though I'm still on the outside looking in.

"Do not neglect to do good and to share what you have, for such sacrifices are pleasing to God.

—Hebrews 13:16

Chapter 10

What I Know Now

"If a free society cannot help the many who are poor, it cannot save the few who are rich."

— John F. Kennedy

"A gentle answer turns away wrath, but a harsh word stirs up anger."

— Proverbs 15:1

I've come to recognize that there are several areas where Cuyahoga County, primarily Cleveland, has the opportunity to differentiate itself.

First, the city of Cleveland has the resources to be an economic powerhouse and destination location. We have some of the brightest people in the nation working to solve some of the toughest problems. Yet, we continue to miss opportunities for greatness. This needs to change.

Second, in order to thrive, we must tackle poverty—both through focusing on safety and education. Years of political infighting have harmed the city's ability to deliver viable safety services. Stronger collaboration among the regional government, city government, and the safety professionals can help turn this around. We must put our children's education at the forefront of our efforts for improvement. Because I've spent years fighting for the academic advancement of Cleveland's kids through programs such as Project Love, I've seen both the problems and our potential up close. It can be done.

Finally, if we view collaboration as a positive instead of a negative, we can continue our progress in economic development across the county and in the city of Cleveland.

For someone like me, who desires significant change to help the greater good of all, my experience running for elected office was positive in that it encouraged me to keep trying to make a change. It is why I continue to do what I do now, even though I'm still on the outside looking in.

I am not a politician. I am not a politician. I am not a politician. I am a leader.

Running for county executive was never about my desire to become a politician or be an officeholder. That's not what I wanted to be. Running for office was a journey of faith. The reason I did it was because I died and was brought back with a sense of purpose to serve the greater good. That drives all of my decisions today. If God left me here to do something else, something different than I was doing before, what was that something else?

I truly believe that running for office was what I was supposed to do, so I did it. I had the skills to do the job. And because I believed I was brought back to do something different, something bigger than what I would normally have done, something for the greater good, I funded my own campaign.

My campaign for county executive cost me more than $1 million. I didn't decide to spend that kind of money because it was lying around. The decision was based on what political experts told me I would have to spend to launch a legitimate campaign. When I announced my candidacy, nobody knew who I was. I was running without a party, so I had to spend that money to make a difference.

Early on, I made a commitment: If I'm going to get into the campaign, I am going to be serious about it. And if I'm going to be serious about it, it is going to cost me $1 million. I didn't have that kind of money in cash. To pay for the campaign, I had to borrow money and liquidate some of my assets.

Shortly before the election, the polls indicated I was not going to win. They proved to be spot on. When I realized that, my friends questioned whether I should spend that last $250,000 in media or just accept the fact that I'd taken my best shot but wasn't going to win.

But I realized I couldn't stop. The forces behind my journey said to me, *"Do all you can do and leave the rest up to God. If it's going to happen, it's going to happen."*

The one thing I knew for sure, I wanted to wake up on Wednesday, Nov. 3, 2010, look at myself in the mirror and know that I had done everything I could, that I'd put it all in.

I didn't want to say to myself, *"That was really dumb. I did all that work and everything was lined up perfectly and I didn't spend that money because I was selfish. I blew it."*

So, it turns out that winning wasn't God's plan. But I wasn't angry when I lost. I was more puzzled than anything. Losing the election must be part of a bigger plan because I don't believe that God's plan was for me to spend a million dollars for nothing. That million dollars could have gone to a lot of different places and done more good. At this point, I'm operating on the belief that I had to spend this money for that purpose, which will take me where I need to go ultimately to work for the greater good of all.

I survived a cardiac arrest.
I've had a good life.
I gave my family a good life.

Now my life is about moving forward and making a difference because I believe that's what I'm here to do. I am so grateful for what I've had. I am doing this because I can and because this is what I know how to do.

Being on the outside of the political establishment, it's frustrating to see what needs to be fixed and see that the people inside don't know how to fix it. They don't seem to know how to break down a problem, find a solution and implement it.

I do.

What I learned about politics during the campaign is that it is very much an entity unto itself. There is a hierarchy, with leaders at the top, and things that trickle down all the way to the people on the street. Groups operate with impunity because they feel that nobody can touch them. If you aren't anointed by the leadership, who are often working quietly behind the scenes, it is very difficult to get in or make a difference.

Ninety percent of candidates endorsed by the party establishment win the election. There are very few things in life like that.

Look at me. I was a political outsider, an Independent and the brother of an organized crime wannabe. I knew what was coming. The very first media story that aired after I announced my candidacy mentioned my brother, Tom, and his conviction for aggravated murder more than 35 years earlier. They didn't mention my business success or philanthropy, but focused on my brother. I knew it was going to be an uphill fight. I could have cared less. He is my brother and I love him.

I spent a lot of time preparing for interviews. I had sat down before with the media for interviews. But when you're running for elected office, the interviews—and the questions—are quite different. I practiced and practiced, so when the interviewer asked me the question about my brother I didn't get angry. I didn't get flustered, and I didn't lose my cool. Given my training, I just dealt with it. Actually, I was thankful that that happened in my first interview because it turned out to be good practice.

Most of my campaign was about taking the high road—being gracious to everybody and eschewing negative campaigning. Aiming below the belt would have been the wrong approach for me and gone against everything I'd worked so hard to build in my life.

On Election Day, Linda and I voted at about 9 a.m. The media was there to film us casting our ballots. Even though I knew by then we weren't going to win, it was a good day. I stayed positive and upbeat; I wore my game face. The contest still had to be played out.

To celebrate the election and all the hard work everyone put in, we had a party at the Masonic Temple. It was the same place where Linda and I had graduated from high school—we had both walked across that stage to receive our diplomas. We played *"The Impossible Dream,"* which was also our high school class song. Being there for the Election Day party was like coming full circle.

Linda and the kids were disappointed, of course. But the thing is, that election didn't define me. It wasn't a career in politics I was pursuing. The whole effort was more about seeing what was around the corner, seeing if being county executive was the thing I was supposed to be doing.

I lost, came in third actually, so I went back to my great life to figure out what was next in my journey of faith.

If *"We, The People,"* cannot get together and agree on one thing—demand our politicians enact real campaign finance reform, funded by only the government—nothing good is going to happen. The price of greed is far more than anyone could have imagined. Many people will say we, the people, can't afford to finance public office campaigns. I advocate that on a federal level we cannot afford not to do so. We, The People, are already paying a price that our children will have to pay for and our grandchildren far into the future.

Following the money will lead you to the answers that we've all been looking for. The problem is pretty simple: The fox is in the chicken coop.

"We can say with some assurance that, although children may be the victims of fate, they will not be the victims of our neglect."
— John F. Kennedy

Epilogue

"Three things will last forever—faith, hope, and love—and the greatest of these is love."

— 1 Corinthians 13:13

The most difficult thing I have encountered in the last three years is getting people to believe that I want to work for the greater good of all. I ran for office to make my community a better place to live, period. My campaign in 2010 and today is based on one fundamental, guiding principle. Whatever I do is guided by Faith, Hope and Love (1 Corinthians 13:13). I believe I am called to work to end the cycle of poverty and violence escalating in our city. Cleveland can be a great destination city; I will work to make that happen.

After the 2010 election was over, and I lost, I wondered why I had gone through that experience. Why did I spend the time to attend more than 1,000 meetings and events; visit more than 60 of the departments and directors within the county system; spend in excess of $1 million of my own money; and run as an independent? I tried to show people that I was not going to be controlled by anybody, and that I would only be held accountable to the greater good of all, which would ultimately benefit everyone.

My soul-searching led me to conclude that this was an experience I needed to have to fully understand the dysfunction in government. I also recognized that good people simply don't have the opportunity to implement solutions on the basis of best practices because they run the risk of bumping heads with the so-called "protected" people in government. And as a result, we have antiquated ideas and antiquated procedures that have stymied efficient operation of government entities.

A few weeks later, I had lunch with a good friend. We discussed the loss, and I explained I wasn't sure where I needed to go from here. He smiled and asked me, *"What do you want to be? Do you want to be a politician, or do you just want to make a difference?"*

"All I want to do is make a difference," I replied.

"Then your answer is simple," he said. *"Take that information and go to the people and the organizations and offer your help and your suggestions."*

This made perfect sense. I didn't want to become a politician to affect change. So, I embarked upon that mission.

But something strange happened—everybody that I tried to speak with was not available. Doors that were open to me as a candidate, were closed now that I was just a businessman.

Some of the people who spoke with me in the past would not speak to me now. Some of the people with whom I spoke and offered ideas and solutions during my run for county executive suddenly told me that they couldn't do anything about those recommendations because of politics. And some of the politicians either refused to speak with me or tried to placate me by listening and then ignoring what we had discussed. A few even acted upon my ideas and implemented plans, now attributed to themselves, that were very similar to those I had provided them with.

And so, I came to a new conclusion: In order to truly make a difference, I did need to get into a position of power. And unfortunately, that meant going back into the political arena.

I also recognized that attempting to foster change as an Independent simply wasn't going to work, so I returned to my original political party designation. People don't care about right or wrong as much as they care about being loyal to a particular party—my last affiliation as a Democrat back in 1982.

My original intent in running for office as an Independent was to demonstrate for everyone that I would be independent of any outside influence. If elected, I would not have been obligated to anyone, except the public, to do the right thing for the greater good of all. After the election I also realized that my Democratic upbringing and values were at the core of what I had always been.

Some people will try to tell you that I am a Republican, and they will say it's because I made a contribution to the McCain-Palin campaign, even though I have provided the facts over and over. There is a back-story to that campaign contribution that few people know.

These are the facts. One of my friend's sons has Down syndrome. He had worked to build a group home for children with Down syndrome, which is a cause I support. Sarah Palin has a child with Down syndrome. During the campaign, she publicly committed herself to supporting that cause.

My friend, who is a life-long Democrat, brought her to town for an event. He asked me to contribute because he knew I also believed in this cause. So I did. If there is one thing people do know about me, I support worthy causes. I don't distinguish whether its a Democrat, Republican or Independent who is supporting that cause; a good cause is a good cause.

That said, over the years I have also donated thousands of dollars to both the Democratic Party and numerous Democratic candidates.

As a result of my unsuccessful effort to implement some of my ideas to transform the city of Cleveland into a vibrant tourist destination, as well as the inability to expand the educational program that I have been involved with for nearly 20 years, Project Love, into the full city school system, I decided to run for office again—this time as the Mayor of Cleveland.

I took a deep dive into the specific issues facing the city. What I found was extremely disturbing.

According to the Ohio Department of Education, the schools are currently in worse shape today than they were eight years ago, in 2006. Their standardized test scores are significantly lower. As of May 2013, the city's murder rate was nearly double for the same time period in 2012. And eight years ago, the poverty rate in the city of Cleveland was 27 percent. Today, it is nearly 35 percent. On the issues that are most important to the residents of Cleveland, the current administration has failed. The city can only be judged by the quality of life of its residents, which is the most important measure on which the mayor of any city should be judged.

So, why did I decide to run for mayor? I have decided that my journey of faith was not to be political, but to be biblical. I've learned that if I want to make a difference, I need to do it from inside City Hall. I truly believe that the journey I've been on for the last six years will culminate with a win on Election Day, November 5, 2013.

> *"Three things will last forever—*
> *faith, hope, and love—and the*
> *greatest of these is love."*
> **— 1 Corinthians 13:13**

Appendix

Excerpts from

"The Dimensions of a Complete Life"
by Martin Luther King, Jr.

Many, many centuries ago, out on a lonely, obscure island called Patmos, a man by the name of John caught a vision of the new Jerusalem descending out of heaven from God. One of the greatest glories of this new city of God that John saw was its completeness. It was not partial and one-sided, but it was complete in all three of its dimensions. And so, in describing the city in the twenty-first chapter of the book of Revelation, John says this: *"The length and the breadth and the height of it are equal." In other words, this new city of God, this city of ideal humanity, is not an unbalanced entity but it is complete on all sides."*

One day the psalmist looked up and noticed the vastness of the cosmic order. He noticed the infinite expanse of the solar system; he noticed the beautiful stars; he gazed at the moon with all its scintillating beauty, and he said in the midst of all of this, *"What is man?"* He comes forth with an answer: *"Thou hast made him a little lower than the angels, and crowned him with glory and honor."*

"Thou hast made him a little less than divine, a little less than God, and crowned him with glory and honor."

O' God, our gracious heavenly Father, we thank thee for the inspiration of Jesus the Christ, who came to this world to show us the way. And grant that we will see in that life the fact that we are made for that which is high and noble and good. Help us to live in line with that high calling, that great destiny. In the name of Jesus we pray.

Amen.

There are three dimensions of any complete life to which we can fitly give the words of this text: length, breadth, and height. The length of life as we shall think of it here is not its duration or its longevity, but it is the push of a life forward to achieve its personal ends and ambitions. It is the inward concern for one's own welfare. The breadth of life is the outward concern for the welfare of others. The height of life is the upward reach for God.

These are the three dimensions of life, and without the three being correlated, working harmoniously together, life is incomplete. Life is something of a great triangle. At one angle stands the individual person, at the other angle stands other persons, and at the top stands the Supreme, Infinite Person, God. These three must meet in every individual life if that life is to be complete.

Now let us notice first the length of life. I have said that this is the dimension of life in which the individual is concerned with developing his inner powers. It is that dimension of life in which the individual pursues personal ends and ambitions. This is perhaps the selfish dimension of life, and there is such a thing as moral and rational self-interest. If one is not concerned about himself he cannot be totally concerned about other selves.

Some years ago, a learned rabbi, the late Joshua Liebman, wrote a book entitled *Peace of Mind*. He has a chapter in the book entitled "Love Thyself Properly." In this chapter he says in substance that it is impossible to love other selves adequately unless you love your own self properly. Many people have been plunged into the abyss of emotional fatalism because they did not love themselves properly. So every individual has a responsibility to be concerned about himself enough to discover what he is made for. After he discovers his calling he should set out to do it with all the strength and power in his being. He should do it as God Almighty called him at this particular moment in history to do it. He should seek to do his job so well that the living, the dead, or the unborn could not do better. No matter how small one thinks his life's work is in terms of the norms of the world and the so-called big jobs, he must realize that it has cosmic significance if he is serving humanity and doing the will of God.

To carry this to one extreme, if it falls your lot to be a street sweeper, sweep streets as Raphael painted pictures, sweep streets as Michelangelo carved marble, sweep streets as Beethoven composed music, sweep streets as Shakespeare wrote poetry. Sweep streets so well that all of the hosts in heaven and earth will have to pause and say, *"Here lived a great street sweeper who swept his job well."* In the words of Douglas Mallock:

> If you can't be a highway, just be a trail;
> If you can't be the sun, be a star;
> For it isn't by size that you win or fail —
> Be the best of whatever you are.

When you do this, you have mastered the first dimension of life—the length of life. But don't stop here. There are some people who never get beyond this first dimension. They are brilliant people; often they do an excellent job in developing their inner powers; but they live as if nobody else lived in the world but themselves. There is nothing more tragic than to find an individual bogged down in the length of life, devoid of the breadth.

The breadth of life is that dimension of life in which we are concerned about others. An individual has not started living until he can rise above the narrow confines of his individualistic concerns to the broader concerns of all humanity.

So often, racial groups are concerned about the length of life, their economic privileged position, their social status. So often, nations of the world are concerned about the length of life, perpetuating their nationalistic concerns, and their economic ends. May it not be that the problem in the world today is that individuals as well as nations have been overly concerned with the length of life, devoid of the breadth? But there is still something to remind us that we are interdependent, that we are involved in a single process, that we are all somehow caught in an inescapable network of mutuality. Therefore, whatever affects one directly affects all indirectly.

As long as there is poverty in the world I can never be rich, even if I have a million dollars. As long as diseases are rampant and millions of people in this world cannot expect to live more than 28 or 30 years, I can never be totally healthy, even if I just got a good check-up at the Mayo Clinic. I can never be what I ought to be until you are what you ought to be. This is the way our world is made. No individual or nation can stand out, boasting of being independent. We are interdependent. So John Donne placed it in graphic terms when he affirmed, *"No man is an island entire of itself. Every man is a piece of a continent, a part of the main."* Then he goes on to say, *"Any man's death diminishes me because I am involved in mankind, and therefore never send to know for whom the bell tolls; it tolls for thee."* When we discover this, we master the second dimension of life.

Finally, there is a third dimension. Some people never get beyond the first two. They develop their inner powers; they love humanity; but they stop right here. They end up with the feeling that man is the end of all things; that humanity is God. Philosophically or theologically, many of them would call themselves humanists. They seek to live life without a sky. They find themselves bogged down on the horizontal plane without being integrated on the vertical plane. But if we are to live the complete life we must reach up and discover God. H.G. Wells was right: *"The man who is not religious begins at nowhere and ends at nothing."*

You look at me and you think you see Martin Luther King. You don't see Martin Luther King; you see my body, but you must understand, my body can't think, my body can't reason. You don't see that me that makes me *"Me".* You can never see my personality.

In a real sense, everything that we see is a shadow cast by that which we do not see. Plato was right: *"The visible is a shadow cast by the invisible."* And so God is still around. All of our new knowledge, all of our new developments, cannot diminish his being one iota. These new advances have banished God neither from the microcosmic compass of the atom nor from the vast, unfathomable ranges of interstellar space. The more we learn about this universe, the more mysterious and awesome it becomes. God is still here.

So I say to you, seek God and discover him and make him a power in your life. Without him, all of our efforts turn to ashes and our sunrises into darkest nights. Without him, life is a meaningless drama with the decisive scenes missing. But with him, we are able to rise from the fatigue of despair to the buoyancy of hope. With him, we are able to rise from the midnight of desperation to the daybreak of joy. Saint Augustine was right—we were made for God and we will be restless until we find rest in him.

Love yourself, if that means rational, healthy, and moral self-interest. You are commanded to do that. That is the length of life. Love your neighbor as you love yourself. You are commanded to do that. That is the breadth of life. But never forget that there is a first and even greater commandment, *"Love the Lord thy God with all thy heart and all thy soul and all thy mind."* This is the height of life. And when you do this, you live the complete life.

Thank God for John who, centuries ago, caught a vision of the new Jerusalem. God grant that those of us who still walk the road of life will catch this vision and decide to move forward to that city of complete life in which the length and the breadth and the height are equal.

O' God, our gracious heavenly Father, we thank thee for all of the insights of the ages, and we thank thee for the privilege of having fellowship with thee. Help us to discover ourselves, to discover our neighbors, and to discover thee, and to make all part of our life. Grant that we will go now with grim and bold determination to live the complete life. In the name and spirit of Jesus, we pray.

Amen.

About the Authors

Ken Lanci

Ken Lanci is a native Clevelander, successful businessman, and philanthropist. He has over 30 years of business experience; growing his own successful printing company and helping other businesses emerge from failure and thrive. When he sees problems, he tackles them, head on. He is driven by one goal, to work for the greater good of his community.

Ken entered politics to take the next step on his journey of faith, to work for the people of his community. He ran for the office of Cuyahoga County executive in 2010 as an independent. He was guided solely by the best interests of the people of Cuyahoga County.

In *Working for the Greater Good of All...Really*, Ken tells his story, from childhood in the mean streets of Cleveland's east side, to learning to be a business man. He talks candidly about his death at age 57 and recovery, which put him on his current journey of faith.

Manya Chylinski

Manya Chylinski is a freelance writer interested in travel, language, culture, education and business. Through her company, Alley424 Communications, she specializes in content development for business clients.

She started her career as a research librarian and has worked as an editor. She lives in Boston, MA.